A Mity Nice History

GARY FLINN

AMERICAN PALATE

Published by American Palate
A Division of The History Press
Charleston, SC
www.historypress.com

KEWPEE® 🐾
KEWPEE WE CATER TO ALL THE FOLKS® 🔆
MARCHOCOLATE®
HAMBURG PICKLE ON TOP! MAKES YOUR HEART GO FLIPPITY FLOP!®
HAMBURG-PICKLE-ON-TOP-MAKES YOUR HEART GO FLIPPITY-FLOP® ▦
FEBRUCHERRY®
KEWPEE HOTELS® 🍔
CLEAN SWEET PRETTY PLUMP KEWPEE WE CATER TO ALL THE FOLKS
    HAMBURG-PICKLE-ON-TOP MAKES YOUR HEART GO FLIPPITY-FLOP.® are
    registered trademarks of Kewpee Inc. ▣

KEWPEE HAMBURGERS is a trademark of Kewpee Inc. 🍔

HALO BURGER® and HALO BURGER HEAVENLY® are registered trademarks of Halo
    Country LLC. ⚫
SEVEN DAYS WITHOUT A HALO BURGER MAKES ONE WEAK! is a trademark of
    Halo Country LLC.

First published 2023

Manufactured in the United States

ISBN 9781467153195

Library of Congress Control Number: 2023932166

Notice: The information in this book is true and complete to the best of our knowledge. It is
offered without guarantee on the part of the author or The History Press. The author and
The History Press disclaim all liability in connection with the use of this book.

In memory of:

*David Kristopeit, who owned Kewpee Lunch of Racine, Wisconsin,
from 1972 to 2003.*

*Frances Thomas Patterson, the widow of Bill Thomas, who owned the original
Kewpee in Flint, Michigan, and broke away from the chain, renaming his
restaurants Halo Burger in 1967.*

CONTENTS

FOREWORDS

Since I was a kid, I wanted to work with my dad in the hustle and bustle downtown. It's like I went to work with him and never looked back. Throughout all my years there, I love what I work for and who I do it for. Our customers are more like family, and you get to watch them grow—it's pretty awesome. Tradition is something we take seriously in this family. I'm the fourth generation, and I have big shoes to fill. My great-grandmother made it through the Great Depression, so it gave me hope through COVID. We all have our obstacles in business, but you push through and keep making burgers.

In 2020, we were invited to Miami to compete in a national competition with the Food Network—to say my dream came true was an understatement because we hadn't even landed in Miami yet. Just simply being invited to the South Beach Wine & Food Festival (SOBEWFF) was a privilege on its own.

A 2016 photo of Gary Weston and his father, Russell Weston, third- and second-generation operators, respectively, of Weston's Kewpee Burger in Lansing, Michigan. Weston's Kewpee is the oldest-surviving Kewpee establishment. *Courtesy of Weston's Kewpee Burger.*

We got to meet Rachael Ray and some professional chefs, and they all got to eat one of our Kewpee burgers—it was a dream! You could only imagine when we heard our name being called as the winners! I cried the walk up to the front because it was all the work from my great-grandmother, my grandpa and my dad. We did it!

I love what I do and our customers, the community that supports us. We are truly blessed. It's easy to come to work every day with an amazing staff—some who have been with us forty-one years. It's not work anymore if it's you doing your dream! One burger at a time.

—Autumn Weston, Fourth-Generation Operator
of Weston's Kewpee in Lansing, Michigan

Halo Burger is one of the oldest hamburger chains in the United States and originated in Flint, Michigan, way back in 1923. Originally called Kewpee, the company served its first hamburger out of a "boxcar"-style wagon on Harrison Street in downtown Flint.

There, we created the world's first "deluxe" hamburger, made with 100 percent fresh, never-frozen beef, pressed on a searing hot grill to give it just the right amount of char. Then we top it with fresh cut tomatoes, lettuce and mayonnaise. That's one deluxe burger!

Now we serve our burgers with "The Works"—lettuce, tomato, onion, pickle, ketchup, mustard and mayonnaise. This is the burger you used to get in your backyard when your parents had Fourth of July parties. It's big, it's juicy and it's topped with hand-cut toppings between a fresh baked bun.

We're also known for our world-famous Olive Burger, which has remained a favorite for generations. Couple this with our signature Boston Cooler, and you'll get the true Halo Burger experience. We're inspired by midwestern foods and flavors, including Vernors ginger ale, Koegel's Hot Dogs, Wisconsin Cheese Curds and more—plus, our customers love it, too.

Halo Burger not only serves up award winning burgers—we also employ about 150 people in Mid-Michigan! Born and raised in Michigan, we value our traditions and are committed to our midwestern legacy. Above and beyond all else, we're in the business of people and proud to be active members within our community.

And remember, "Seven Days without a Halo Burger Makes One Weak!"

—Domenique Annoni, marketing manager at Halo Burger
(the former Kewpee) in Flint, Michigan

A 1943 vintage photo showing Walter Block (*bottom center*), who owned the Kewpee in Racine, Wisconsin, from 1930 to 1957. The other people in the photo are unidentified. *Courtesy of Trudy Kristopeit.*

The Racine Kewpee has been an integral part of my life and the history of my family. I started working there well before it was legal at about ten years of age, and I am now seventy-three. But before then, my uncle and aunt owned it, and I remember going there on Sunday each year after my church's children's Christmas festival, probably starting when I was four.

But more than this, this Kewpee is an integral part of the city of Racine history. After all, the Kewpee will be one hundred years old in 2026. Everyone knows where the Kewpee is and what it means to Racine. Downtown Racine would not be the same today without the presence of the Kewpee, and I am proud to have been a part of it so long.

—David Kristopeit of Kewpee in Racine, Wisconsin,
of blessed memory

My father, Gerald D. Boyles, purchased a Kewpee Hotel restaurant from Samuel Blair on October 1, 1929. The restaurant was located in downtown Grand Rapids and was successfully operated until February 15,

1958, when my father unexpectedly died. That was the date when I began my Kewpee management responsibilities on behalf of my mother, who had inherited the restaurant following my father's death.

I managed the Kewpee operations until 1970, when the four Kewpee locations were merged into Mr. Fables Systems Inc., a corporation owned by my partner and first cousin Richard A. Faber and myself. The fourteen Mr Fables restaurants located in West Michigan were sold in 1988.

I fondly remember going to the Grand Rapids downtown location with my dad and doing odd clean-up jobs. The store was closed on Sundays. As a young boy, I worked every summer vacation and continued that schedule in high school and college. I learned nearly every operation from dishwashing and janitorial cleaning to carhopping, food prep and fry cook. I loved my experiences and recruited several of my best friends to also work at Kewpees. I also very much enjoyed interacting with customers and our well-trained and friendly staff.

I am eagerly awaiting Gary Flinn's new book on the history of Kewpee Hotels restaurants.

—John Boyles, former operator of Kewpee/Mr. Fables
of Grand Rapids, Michigan

PREFACE

In 1916 in Wichita, Kansas, Walter Anderson opened his first diner in a converted streetcar. In the process of trying to cook ground meat faster, he developed his version of the hamburger. He added holes in the patty to make it cook faster and used rolls as buns to create what we now know as the slider. He partnered with insurance and real estate salesman Billy Ingram to create the hamburger chain with the full name White Castle System of Eating Houses Corporation, with the short name being White Castle. In order to assure patrons that White Castle's food was good, the interior and exterior of its locations were painted white, and the staff wore white clothing to evoke that the locations were clean and sanitary. Ingram would later buy out Anderson's interest in the company and had to endure competition from imitators cashing in on White Castle's success. He successfully sued the most blatant imitator, White Tower, forcing that chain to change its restaurants' design. White Castle is still owned by the Ingram family.

Kewpee is the second-oldest hamburger restaurant chain behind White Castle, which was founded in 1921. Kewpee Hotel founder Samuel V. Blair named the hamburger stand he established in 1923 in Flint, Michigan, after its mascot, the Kewpie doll, inspired by that doll's popularity. Flint is nicknamed the "Vehicle City" because of its factories, which made horse-drawn carriages and later evolved to manufacture motor vehicles. Buick was the first notable automaker to establish a factory in Flint. General Motors, which evolved from Buick, was founded in Flint. General Motors founder Billy Durant also founded Chevrolet, which became part of General Motors.

The Kewpie doll was the creation of cartoonist and illustrator Rose O'Neill in 1909, inspired by baby Cupid illustrations she introduced in *Ladies' Home Journal* magazine. Her illustrations of these babies appeared in popular comic pages titled *Kewpieville*, which appeared in *Ladies' Home Journal*, *Woman's Home Companion* and *Good Housekeeping* magazines. The popularity of Kewpie dolls led to O'Neill designing paper dolls, which evolved into actual dolls.

O'Neill was generous with her friends. While she never apparently legally protected the Kewpie name or the doll, according to the *Muncie Evening*

Opposite: Kewpie doll creator Rose O'Neill. *Courtesy of the Library of Congress.*

Left: *Kewpieville* comic page by Rose O'Neill from the May 1926 issue of *Ladies' Home Journal. Public domain from Google Books.*

Press—Muncie, Indiana, had a Kewpee location next to the newspaper's office—she authorized and was executing the designs of signs for Kewpee Hotel locations. She was a writer, poet, illustrator and sculptor with homes in New England and Missouri. Her Missouri home is today the Bonniebrook Museum, devoted to her legacy.

In order to trademark the name, Blair altered the spelling to *Kewpee*. At the time he founded Kewpee, he was already middle aged at around fifty-three in 1923. With the success of his Kewpee Hotel hamburger stand on Harrison Street and its burgers, he began licensing the use of the Kewpee trademarks of the name and the doll design, plus use of his design for his hamburger wrappers and napkins. But each separately owned location had its own menu and own style of hamburger. The oldest-surviving licensee is in Lansing, Michigan, which is now on its fourth generation of management by the Weston family.

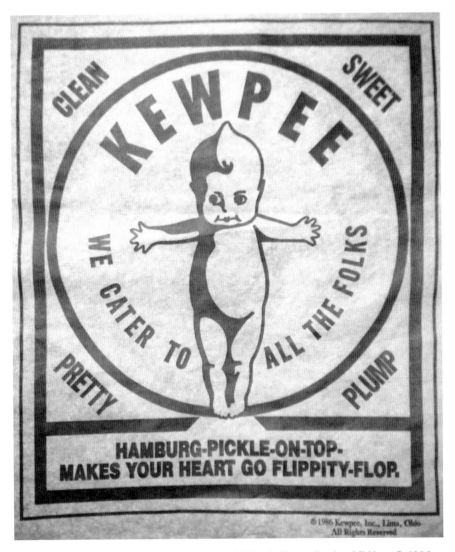

The famous Kewpee burger wrapper. *Courtesy of Weston's Kewpee, Lansing, Michigan, © 1986, Kewpee Inc.*

Blair himself created Kewpee Hotel's slogan, which, according to the United States Patent and Trademark Office, was first used in 1924: "Hamburg pickle on top! Makes your heart go flippity-flop!"

In 1926, an energetic young man of around twenty-two named Edwin Adams opened his own Kewpee Hotel stand in Toledo, Ohio. He not only opened his own hamburger stand but also had ambitions to open and license additional Kewpee Hotel locations in different cities. It seemed that the aging founder, Samuel Blair, known as Old Man Kewpee, was content to concentrate on his successful hamburger stand in Flint, which expanded into a full-sized restaurant. So Blair sold the rights to the Kewpee Hotel trademarks to Adams in 1926.

When Adams bought the rights from O'Neill for use of the Kewpie doll image as Kewpee Hotel's mascot, she had one stipulation. The Kewpie doll's wings had to be clipped. That is why the Kewpie doll logo on burger wrappers is wingless.

It was boasted in earlier books that mentioned Kewpee restaurants that at the chain's peak there were around four hundred locations just before World War II and the number of restaurants shrank due to wartime meat shortages. But it seems that the four hundred number was an exaggeration. In tabulating the number of Kewpee locations past and present, only forty-four communities could be identified has having at least one Kewpee hamburger stand or restaurant. Of the forty-four identified communities, only three still have Kewpee locations in operation. Three are at Kewpee's current home base of Lima, Ohio, and there are one each in Lansing, Michigan, and Racine, Wisconsin. The original Kewpee Hamburgs in Flint had two locations in 1967 when it split off from Kewpee and was renamed Halo Burger. The second Kewpee in Flint is still in operation as Halo Burger and gives its founding year as Kewpee's founding year of 1923.

When my editor for The History Press, John Rodrigue, asked me to write a book about popular food in the Flint area, my first thought was the Flint-style Coney Island hot dog. While I included a chapter on the Coney Island restaurants located in downtown Flint in my first book, *Remembering Flint, Michigan*, I knew that Dave Liske had already written a book for The History Press titled *The Flint Coney: A Savory History*, published in 2022. My other thought was Flint's Halo Burger restaurants celebrating their centennial in 2023. So that became my choice for my fourth History Press book. Halo Burger began as the first Kewpee Hotel founded by Sam Blair, which developed into a chain of licensed Kewpee restaurants, mainly in the Midwest. The five Kewpee restaurants still in operation are either celebrating Kewpee's centennial in 2023 or their own centennials later in the decade. This gave me an opportunity to write a book not only of local interest to Flint residents and expatriates but also of regional interest in the Midwest—not only in Lima, but also in Lansing and Racine, where there are still Kewpee restaurants in operation. Plus the numerous towns, large and small, which used to have at least one Kewpee restaurant or hamburger stand.

ACKNOWLEDGEMENTS

Putting together this book has been a group effort with several individuals and institutions helping out. I'll begin with the operators of the five Kewpee restaurants. They are Harrison and Scott Shutt in Lima, Ohio; Gary and Autumn Weston in Lansing, Michigan; and Richard and Andrew Buehrens along with Trudy Kristopeit and her late husband, David, in Racine, Wisconsin.

Thanks also goes to my contact at Flint Kewpee successor restaurant Halo Burger, marketing manager Domenique Annoni, along with former Halo Burger employee Kim Leser. Thanks also to John Boyles, who operated the Kewpee/Mr. Fables restaurants in Grand Rapids, Michigan.

Among the libraries helping out were the Flint Public Library, the Toledo Lucas County Public Library; the Forest Parke Libraries and Archives–Capital Area District Libraries serving the Lansing, Michigan area; Michigan State University Library; Grand Rapids Public Library; Kalamazoo Public Library; the Findlay-Hancock County Public Library; and the St. Joseph County Public Library, South Bend, Indiana.

Also the Grand Rapids History Center, the Kalamazoo Valley Museum, the M-Live Media Group, the Sloan Museum Archives and the Internet Archive.

Other individuals who helped out include Jason Mancuso, Brent Gillespie, Joel Rash, Wendy All and Karen Tepin-Wresinski, and a very special thanks to Lansing, Michigan historian Timothy Bowman. Bowman helped in finding material in newspapers.com as well as the various city directories found on ancestry.com in finding Kewpee locations in various cities. To aid in developing this book, I created a Facebook page titled "The Kewpee/Halo Burger Centennial Project," which is a clearinghouse for followers to provide their contributions to the book as well as a way for readers to critique my work in progress. Using that Facebook page, I made contact with the "OldToledo" Facebook page seeking info on the Kewpee Hotel locations in Toledo, and along with finding postings previously made about the Toledo Kewpee restaurants, I posted an early draft of the Kewpee in Toledo piece and received useful information to fill out that piece. The "Love Findlay History" Facebook page members gave me enough information to write the brief piece about the Kewpee Hotel that was located in Findlay, Ohio.

If I missed anyone else, I apologize.

Gary Flinn, March 2023

1

KEWPEE FOUNDER
SAMUEL V. BLAIR

Samuel Vincent Blair was born in Rushville, Indiana, on June 15, 1870, the son of Irish immigrants Joseph Blair and Anne Smart Blair. He held several jobs through the years. He studied horticulture and operated orchards. For thirty years, he worked as an iron molder, most notably for the Kalamazoo Stove Company. He also worked as a salesman selling vacuum cleaners and life insurance.

In 1923, he moved to Flint and opened a hamburger stand called the Kewpee Hotel, even though it did not offer lodging, operating out of a wagon at 415 Harrison Street near Kearsley Street behind the post office that stood on Kearsley. That hamburger stand was successful, so it was added onto; by 1928, it was in a large enough building for the establishment to have a telephone.

As the 1920s progressed, Blair began licensing rights for other operators to open Kewpee Hotel Hamburgs hamburger stands and restaurants. Each operator had its own menu and its own style of hamburger. Blair credited himself with inventing the flat bun, the deluxe hamburger and the Olive Burger, which some other Kewpee restaurants also offered. He also claimed credit for introducing curbside and later drive-through service. What the Kewpee Hotel restaurants had in common was the name, the Kewpie doll mascot and the hamburger wrapper bearing the naked Kewpie doll logo along with two slogans: "We cater to all the folks" and "Hamburg pickle on top! Makes your heart go flippity-flop!"

Kewpee Hotel founder Samuel V. Blair, "Old Man Kewpee." *Courtesy of M-Live Media Group.*

In 1926, Blair sold the rights to the Kewpee name and trademarks to Edwin Adams, based in Toledo, Ohio. By World War II, it was written that there were four hundred Kewpee Hotel restaurants and hamburger stands. This made Old Man Kewpee, as Blair was nicknamed, the Hamburger King. But his private life had become complicated. He was married five times. But his short-lived fourth marriage in 1940 was the subject of scandal and made the news.

Blair, who by that time had amassed $500,000 selling hamburgers, according to a 1941 article published in Hearst's *American Weekly*, married his fourth wife, Betty, who was fifty years younger than him, on November 9, 1940, in Toledo, Ohio. It was Betty's third marriage. That was not long after he was granted a divorce from his third wife, Opal. The honeymoon was a multicity whirlwind trip with stops in Flint, up north to the Upper Peninsula and westward to California and Honolulu. Blair's previous wife Opal tagged along for the honeymoon.

In Flint, at the Athletic Club, the newlyweds drank heavily, with champagne flowing. At the hotel in Upper Michigan, Betty took offense to her new husband maintaining his false teeth in public after each course in the meal at the restaurant. In Los Angeles, Betty spent time in that city's hot spots without Sam or Opal. She was thoroughly intoxicated and was found in the arms of a young man. In Honolulu, she allegedly fell in love with an army captain.

Needless to say, Sam filed for divorce. In the divorce hearings, it was found that Sam had a diary that he started keeping twenty-one years before, which helped provide his testimony. The testimony indicated that Betty treated Opal as a mother, and Opal treated Betty like a daughter. Opal knew Betty for six years. While Betty was hoping to get a good chunk of Sam's fortune, Judge Crampton granted Sam's divorce plea and ignored Betty's countersuit. Sam was ordered to pay Betty $1,000 plus $400 in attorneys' fees and to finish an $8,500 house he had started to build for her.

When Sam arrived in Flint in 1923, he had $16.85 on him. On March 29, 1944, at age seventy-three, he announced his retirement as owner of the Kewpee Hotel on Harrison Street, effective April 1. So a huge retirement

The original Kewpee Hotel hamburger stand on Harrison Street in Flint, Michigan. *Courtesy of Halo Burger.*

party in the Athletic Club lounge was held on Friday night, March 31. He stated that Flint was very good to him. But he hated to admit that he was born in Indiana. "Imagine being associated with [Wendell] Willkie!" (Willkie was the 1940 presidential candidate who lost to Franklin D. Roosevelt.) About his retirement, Blair stated, "From now on, it will be a vacation until I die. I shall never forget how good Flint has been to me." As for his restaurant valued at $50,000, he gave a long-term lease to his longtime manager Bill Thomas.

Blair was in Albion visiting his nephew Donald Sampson when he was stricken with a heart attack. He died at Sheldon Memorial Hospital at 5:00 a.m. on Saturday, April 14, 1945, at age seventy-four. Blair's funeral was held the following Tuesday at the Algoe-Gundry chapel in Flint. His body was cremated, and he wished for his ashes to "be scattered from an airplane over the residential section of the City of Flint." But he does have a grave marker in Albion at Riverside Cemetery.

According to the obituary published in Albion, he was survived by his wife Rose, three sons and a sister. The sons—Robert of Flint, Francis of

Kalamazoo (who operated his own Kewpee Hotel there) and Theodore of Northville—split equally their father's estate estimated at $30,000 in real estate and $1,000 in personal property. The will provided that Blair's Kewpee Hotel property at 415 Harrison Street be held in trust until his youngest grandchild reached voting age, when it would be sold and the proceeds divided among all the grandchildren. Bill Thomas bought it in 1958.

The *Flint Journal* report regarding Samuel Blair's estate worth around $31,000 conflicts with the wealth reported in a September 7, 1941 full-page article titled "Headache Honeymoon of Mr. Blair, Hamburger Hero," published in the *American Weekly*, a Sunday supplement inserted in Hearst newspapers, including the *Detroit Times*.

The complete article from the *American Weekly* is on display at the Kewpee location in Racine, Wisconsin, and the complete text of the piece follows.

2

HEADACHE HONEYMOON OF MR. BLAIR, HAMBURGER HERO

This is the complete article published in the September 7, 1941 issue of the American Weekly *and is presented here by special arrangement with Hearst Communications Inc., Hearst Newspapers Division. The writer of this story was not credited.*

"A Pickle on top make the heart go FLIPPITY FLOP!"

Having had three wives but still hanging on to half a million dollars made by selling hamburgers each with a pickle on top, Mr. Samuel V. Blair of Flint, Michigan, was entitled to peaceful retirement at the age of 71.

But he neglected to do so.

Instead of simplifying his affairs, he announced that life had began all over for him and that he was going to ride the moon.

The inspiration for this ambition was a lady just 50 years younger than himself, who became his fourth wife, Mrs. Betty Blair.

Betty, though scarcely old enough to vote, had been married twice before and supposed that this moon rodeo idea, referred in the high time they would have on their honeymoon.

Also Betty says that he promised to make her independently wealthy. Therefore the very day she received her second divorce, which was financed by Mr. Blair, Betty told him to bring on his moony honeymoon.

And he did.

"A pickle on top makes the heart go flippity-flop" is the slogan which made the Hamburger King rich. It was the inspiration of his life. The pickle feature made all the girls fall for his hamburger which is shaped somewhat like a full moon.

But it proved to be a poor idea when applied to a honeymoon.

Above: Article from the September 7, 1941 issue of the *American Weekly. Courtesy of Hearst Communications Inc., Hearst Newspapers division.*

Opposite: "Samuel V. Blair, the 71-Year-Old Inventor of the "Kewpee" Hamburger With The Pickle on Top, Who Was Awarded a Divorce." *Courtesy of Hearst Communications Inc., Hearst Newspapers division.*

Samuel V. Blair, the 71-Year-Old Inventor of the "Kewpee"
Hamburger With the Pickle on Top, Who
Was Awarded a Divorce.

According to all concerned, this honeymoon was a thoroughly "pickled" one with no doubts except as to which party to the strange proceedings drank the most.

The result was worse than a common nightmare. It was more like a delirium tremens, because the trip was, in a manner of speaking, chaperoned by Mrs. Opal Smith who, not so long ago, had been the third Mrs. Blair.

The 47-year-old Mrs. Smith, however, was no alcoholic hallucination, but actually present in the flesh. She does not seem to have crashed the party and yet who invited her is vague, like most things, "seen through a glass darkly."

In the divorce suit and counter-suit which logically followed such an illogical situation, some said it was the elderly bridegroom while others blamed it on Betty, the blushing bride for the third time.

Anyhow, it was Mr. Blair who paid $500 traveling expenses for this unusual "excess baggage," so it must have been his idea.

But then he complains that Betty slept with Opal every night, so maybe it was her idea.

Opal insists that both invited her and she merely went along because it provided free transportation in the direction of Alaska.

How can any sober person figure it out?

The mystery seems to have been too deep for Circuit Judge Louis C. Cramton of Flint. In granting the divorce to the Hamburger Merchant, together with a few financial crumbs to Betty, the judge criticized all three and referred to Mrs. Opal Smith as "the most unusual figure in the case."

According to the evidence, Betty's divorce decree became final on November 9, 1940, and that very day the pair was united on bonds of matrimony across a gulf of half a century. The moment was done, at Toledo, Ohio, they hurried to Flint where the "pickle" appeared in a grand celebration at the Flint Athletic Club.

On the witness stand Mr. Blair admitted that he became "very intoxicated" and admitted as much for his bride.

Somehow, they got from the club to the train which was to take them to the Pacific Coast. In this alcoholic fog, with taxis, porters, railroad stations and such things looming up, it is hardly fair to expect a plausible explanation of how and when Opal got into the sequence.

Flint is world-famous as the city of sit-down strikes, but there is no foundation to the rumor that Mrs. Smith was sitting in on her ex-husband's

"One of the Hamburger King's 'Kewpee' Stands Made Famous and Profitable by an Extra Pickle With Each Hamburger." (Author's note—This looks to be the Kewpee Hotel restaurant on Harrison Street in Flint as it originally looked.) *Courtesy of Hearst Communications Inc., Hearst Newspapers division.*

fourth honeymoon, in protest against a divorce lockout. She wasn't sabotaging the Hamburger Magnate's next marriage because she had been invited and an invitation accompanied by $500 is a mighty cordial one.

When Opal appeared to them, there was no need for introductions. Mr. Blair and the third Mrs. Blair were all too well acquainted but it seems that the bride had also known her several years before she met Mr. Blair.

In fact Betty testified that her friend Opal had been striving for some time to have them meet.

In such a pickled condition most anything could happen, and perhaps it is not surprising that the bride stumbled into Opal's sleeping compartment, thus spending the bridal night not with the bridegroom, but with his last previous wife.

The late A.H. Woods would have accepted this situation as the first act of one of his famous bedroom farces and started the next act with three awful headaches. In this case there were probably only two. Opal, who was

"The Honeymoon, Like Mr. Blair's Hamburgers, Was Thoroughly 'Pickled.' It Was More Than Ordinary Nightmare, It Carried Out Mr. Blair's Promise of Riding to the Moon, With the Third Mrs. Blair Chaperoning The Hamburger Hero's Fourth Bride." To the right of this drawing, the article read: "Like His Sandwiches Whose 'Pickle on Top Makes the Heart Go Flippity Flop,' His Fourth Wife, 50 Years His Junior, Turned Their Wedding Trip Topsy-Turvy by Inviting His Third Wife Along—And Things Got in Such a Pickle That They Wound Up in Divorce Court." *Courtesy of Hearst Communications Inc., Hearst Newspapers division.*

not at the Athletic Club celebration, says she was perfectly sober and the other two were not in condition for accurate observation.

As often as the pair sobered up both halves seem to have rushed back into pickle again, according to testimony from both sides. Betty says that Samuel did the heaviest drinking but he gives his little bride credit for "nine-tenths of it," and spending her time on the Coast at dances and bars.

"Once," he reminisced, "she tried every drink the bartender could mix."

With so much imbibing, it seemed clear that alcoholic cruelty could not be entirely on one side.

But there were other charges and complaints. The husband waking up in the morning after the bridal night before, remembered that he had just gotten married again, located his misplaced bride and asked that the error be corrected on the next and all succeeding nights.

In spite of his protests, he complained that Betty kept right on sleeping with Opal. Brides have been known to go home to mother the very next day which is embarrassing enough, but for one to go back to the bridegroom's last previous wife was something Mr. Blair contended was unheard of. He was justly annoyed.

The bride admitted that though turning up fairly regularly at his board, for food and drink, she had deserted his bed.

Mrs. Betty Blair, Fourth and Now Disengaged Bride of Mr. Blair. Her Heart Went Flippity-Flop But Not in Rhythm With That of Her Husband.

Opal Smith, Mr. Blair's Third Wife, Who Went Along on His Fourth Honeymoon.

Left: "Mrs. Betty Blair, Fourth and Now Disengaged Bride of Mr. Blair. Her Heart Went Flippity-Flop But Not In Rhythm With That of Her Husband." *Courtesy of Hearst Communications Inc., Hearst Newspapers division.*

Right: "Opal Smith, Mr. Blair's Third Wife, Who Went Along on His Fourth Honeymoon." *Courtesy of Hearst Communications Inc., Hearst Newspapers division.*

But there had been reasons. Sam's attentions, she said, made her sick, especially on account of his false teeth.

She charged that in dining cars and swanky restaurants, it was his "terrible habit" between courses to pull out his uppers with toothpick and napkin to give them a cleaning.

It did not help any for him to point out that she powdered her nose and painted her lips right at the table, which he contended was also a "bathroom job." Sam just made her sick.

The Hamburger Magnate, like most successful business men, had learned that honesty is the best policy and his frankness on the witness stand, no doubt helped win his case. Though spectators in the courtroom at Flint almost had hysterics, he admitted his unconventional table tricks in the following words:

"Yes, I took them (the teeth) out in a hotel and gave them a cleaning at the table. She got pretty mad and I agreed maybe it wasn't the proper thing to do. Food gets in my uppers, though, and I have do something about it. After she complained I used to excuse myself from the table and clean them in private or else I stopped eating."

After all, these wretchedly-fitting uppers were what really ought to have them named as co-respondent it would seem.

Also the bride should have suspected that a man in his seventies, even one who did not specialize in pre-chewed food, like hamburgers, might have "store teeth."

No false-teeth charge could be as weighty in the eyes of the law as Mr. Blair's accusation that Mrs. Blair the Fourth had been false to her marriage vows, which is wrong at age 21 or 71.

Blair complained that in Los Angeles, Betty was missing not only from his bed but even Opal's for two successive nights and all he could find about it was that she had spent much time at some of the hotter hot spots which was no consolation.

Mr. Blair mentions an occasion when he came upon his bride actually in the arms of an ardent young man. After persuading the youth to relinquish his treasure to its lawful owner, the Hamburger King said he had to carry his fourth queen to bed. If pickled to such a state of unconsciousness as this would imply, Betty could hardly have been conscious of infidelity if there was any.

While they were in Honolulu, Blair alleged that his wife fell in love with an army captain.

He said that the captain and Betty came to him with the information that they were in love with each other. According to him, she proposed a divorce which he was to pay for but with only a property settlement of $500, which she seemed to think was a bargain for a rich man whose wife was leaving him.

He said he sadly agreed to the settlement.

Betty told a different story, asserted that it was Blair himself who proposed she walk out with only that stingy pay-off of $500.

The witness whose testimony was heard in dumbfounded silence, was Mrs. Opal Smith, wife number three, who threw the following light on the strange relationship:

"Betty called me Mum,'" she stated, "and I called her, 'Daughter.' I have known Betty for six years and have always regarded her as my daughter. I disapproved of her marriage to Sam. I would not have picked him for her. Had he been a young man I would not have minded so much.

"It was really at Betty's insistence that I went along. She knew I wanted to visit my son in Alaska and it was through Betty that Sam advanced me the $500 for the trip. I left them at Los Angeles and they went on to Honolulu."

Betty placidly testified that her friend, Mrs. Smith, had urged her to try and get some of the Hamburger Fortune, since everyone else was grabbing after it. Sam must have been a shy and wary bird because Betty said that Opal tried for two or three years to get her to meet him.

Next to false teeth, Betty's most serious complaint seems to have been Samuel's jealousy which, according to testimony, was not without some foundation. In a letter introduced as evidence against her, Betty assertedly wrote to a friend as follows:

"As far as his returning to Flint to get a divorce, I don't mind because anywhere he gets it is all right by me as I certainly can't stand his jealousy any longer. I am not surprised at his other wives not living with him. Who could?"

Judge Cramton granted Samuel's divorce plea, ignoring Betty's counter-suit, but ordered him to pay her $1,000, twice the price of freedom mentioned in Honolulu, $400 more in attorneys' fees and to finish an $8,500 house he had started to build for her.

Few hard-working men are as well off as Betty at the age of twenty-one, yet the judge stated that neither she nor Blair was "a fit candidate for marriage."

Apparently the judge himself had been to Honolulu as he pointed out that to the best of his knowledge the climate of the islands was not such as "to change one's love to distaste for her husband in so short a time." He added:

"She knew she was not marrying youth, but was getting financial security, that would make up for the lack of youth, but she wasn't willing to pay the price."

A pickle on top certainly seems to make the heart go flippity flop.

But who got the pickle, Betty or Sam?

DISCLAIMER—As previously mentioned, the preceding article's claim that Blair had a $500,000 fortune in 1941 conflicts with the *Flint Journal's* 1945 article estimating Blair's estate at the time of his death at $31,000.

3

KEWPEE OWNERSHIP HISTORY

T he same year Sam Blair opened his Kewpee Hotel hamburger stand in Flint, he began licensing the Kewpee name and trademark to other hamburger establishments, including the oldest-surviving Kewpee licensee in Michigan's capital city of Lansing, which opened in 1924. As mentioned, Edwin Adams not only opened his own Kewpee stand in Toledo, Ohio, but he also acquired from Blair the rights to the Kewpee name and trademarks in 1926. By the end of the 1920s, between Blair's own Kewpee Hotel locations and locations he licensed, there were more than two hundred locations by the end of the 1920s. It was claimed that at its peak around World War II, there were around four hundred Kewpee locations in Michigan, Illinois, Indiana, Wisconsin, Ohio and New York. Both Blair and Adams made it a point to avoid opening locations in major cities and located their stands in smaller cities outside the mainstream. The number of locations slowly declined for several reasons, including the effects of the Great Depression and wartime meat shortages.

Edwin F. Adams, operator of Kewpee Hotel restaurant locations in Toledo and Akron, Ohio, as well as in a few other cities, including Utica, New York, collected the licensing fees. Back in Flint, Bill Thomas was paying rent to the Blair estate for the original restaurant on Harrison Street and in 1951 opened a second Kewpee location in downtown Flint at the former Vernor's ginger ale sandwich shop. Thomas acquired the original Kewpee location on Harrison Street from the Blair estate in 1958.

Edwin Adams commissioned Kewpee Hotel exterior design for his downtown Toledo, Ohio location that inspired other Kewpee Hotel restaurant designs. *From Pyramid Snap On Mouldings brochure.*

Interior design for downtown Toledo Kewpee Hotel. *From Pyramid Snap On Mouldings brochure.*

In 1967, Adams began to demand a full franchising arrangement and a percentage of the profits. Locations that objected either closed or changed their names. The original Kewpee location in Flint as well as Thomas's second Kewpee location changed their names to Halo Burger.

After Adams died in 1974, his widow, Hortense, took over the rights to the Kewpee name. In 1977, she sold her Kewpee restaurants and the rights to the Kewpee trademarks to two real estate developers who owned apartment buildings, Robert L. Dame and Robert J. Lloyd. By 1981, Kewpee was owned by R&R Investment Corporation. Ownership of the Kewpee trademark was transferred in 1985 from Kewpee of Toledo, which was closing, to Kewpee in Lima, Ohio, managed by Harrison Shutt. He and his son Scott run Kewpee today. Kewpee has three locations in Lima. There are two other Kewpee locations, which are franchisees: Weston's Kewpee in Lansing, Michigan, and the Kewpee Sandwich Shop in Racine, Wisconsin.

THE FIRST KEWPEE BECOMES HALO BURGER

William V. "Bill" Thomas came to Flint in 1933 and started working for Sam Blair in 1938 and eventually became manager. On April 1, 1944, Thomas took over the operations of the very first Kewpee Hotel location started by Blair at 415 Harrison Street in downtown Flint. Thomas leased the restaurant from Blair upon the founder's retirement. Thomas continued to lease the restaurant from Blair's estate after his death in 1945. Bill Thomas's older brother Shelley often worked behind the counter at Kewpee and had a colorful personality, unlike his brother. While Bill was quite a serious person, Shelley was quite the opposite. When a customer gave a $1.25 order to Shelley, he would often reply, "That will be $125.00." An old Kewpee/Halo Burger employee recalled that Shelley always made her day, and she was so happy to see him come into work. She added, "Such a sweet old guy. Had us laughing all the time. Memories." In 1950, Thomas added French fries to the Kewpee menu. Thomas added a second Kewpee location in downtown Flint in 1951 when he bought the Vernor's sandwich shop. It sold Vernor's ginger ale, which the restaurant continues to offer today.

In 1953, Bill Thomas's son Terry began working for his father after school and on weekends, chopping onions and peeling potatoes to make French fries.

Above: Original Kewpee location in Flint on Harrison Street after the restaurant was remodeled. *Courtesy of Halo Burger.*

Opposite, top: Kewpee of Flint owner Bill Thomas (who changed the name of his Kewpee restaurants to Halo Burger in 1967) and his son Terry, who took over Halo Burger after his father's death. *Courtesy of Kim Leser.*

Opposite, bottom: A 1951 photo of Kewpee Hamburgs No. 2 in Flint after taking over the Vernor's Ginger Ale outlet. *Courtesy of Halo Burger.*

Thomas took full ownership of the original Kewpee restaurant in 1958. But back in 1926, Blair sold the rights to the Kewpee name and trademark to another Kewpee restaurant operator in Ohio, Edwin Adams. So Thomas was paying Adams for the rights to use the Kewpee name. In the early 1960s, Adams wanted to switch from a flat royalty fee to a full franchising arrangement. Around that time, Terry Thomas, after completing college, joined his father full time in running the Kewpee Hamburgs restaurants. In 1967, Adams demanded a percentage of the profits from each Kewpee in place of the licensing fees without providing additional support.

Because Bill Thomas did his own advertising and promotion for his Kewpee restaurants, he decided to change the name. On May 12, 1967,

The flagship Halo Burger restaurant in downtown Flint and only surviving former Kewpee in Flint as it looks today. *Author photo*.

the Flint Kewpee restaurants were renamed Bill Thomas' Halo Burger restaurants. Only the name changed. Everything else, including the food, remained the same. The Kewpie doll mascot was replaced by a cow's head with a halo over it with the single-word slogan "Heavenly." The flagship Kewpee burger was renamed the Q.P. burger, standing for "quarter pound" and still offered Olive Burgers, which it still does today. A more notable slogan Halo Burger adopted was "Seven days without a Halo Burger makes one weak." Bill Thomas died on Christmas Eve 1973, the same year Halo Burger expanded outside of downtown Flint with its third location at 3388 South Linden Road, across from the Genesee Valley Center southwest of the city.

Terry took over management of his father's Halo Burger restaurants. Under his management, Halo Burger expanded at its peak to thirteen locations in and around Flint by the 1990s. But sadly, the Harrison Street Halo Burger location, which was the very first Kewpee, fell victim to the development of the University of Michigan–Flint downtown campus and was torn down in 1979 to make way for a parking lot.

The economic downturn the Flint area went through in the late 1980s and early 1990s forced some belt tightening involving layoffs and a reduction

Kewpee Hamburgs of Flint ad before conversion to Halo Burger in 1967. *Courtesy of Flint Public Library.*

Halo Burger ad after changing its name from Kewpee in 1967. *Courtesy of Flint Public Library.*

in employee benefits, but Halo Burger was able to keep its existing locations open. Halo would not add additional locations for about a decade. Terry Thomas stated in a 1997 interview, "We've looked at going national, having talked with people who wanted to buy us out, but we decided to keep it as a family operation." Halo Burgers were able to compete successfully against the national burger chains such as McDonald's, Burger King and Wendy's, and they kept up with some of the fast-food industry trends. Owners added indoor playgrounds to two locations, for example, to appeal to families.

A baseball team Halo Burger co-sponsored (with Foutch Auto Wash) won the 2001 American Amateur Baseball Congress's Stan Musial World Series. The Halo-Foutch team was almost one of six teams to win back-to-back national titles before losing in the 2002 semifinals. The 2001–2 Halo-Foutch teams were enshrined in the Greater Flint Area Sports Hall of Fame.

Down to nine locations in 2010, when it became apparent that the next generation of the Thomas family was not interested in managing Halo Burger, Terry Thomas reluctantly sold the chain to Dortch Enterprises, a franchisee of Subway restaurants in the area, for $10 million. It was a move that Thomas regretted. Thomas had hoped to sell the company to some key employees, but they were unable to secure the necessary bank financing. Dortch was considering picking up the local franchise rights for Sonic Drive-ins but considered buying Halo Burger a more attractive opportunity. President Lou Dortch Jr. stated in 2014, "We liked that it was Michigan based and ninety years old. Why bring in something from out of state when we could take this?" To help in the transition, Terry Thomas was retained as a consultant. Other managers also stayed on, but a handful of redundant office employees were laid off. Dortch had hopes of turning Halo Burger into a national brand. It did open a combination Halo Burger and Subway restaurant in the Flint suburb of Burton along with six new Halo Burger locations outside the Flint area in the Detroit suburbs and in Lansing. But that did not pan out. So in 2015, Dortch put Halo Burger on the market.

The following year, Halo Burger with its fifteen locations was sold to a pair of Detroit-area entrepreneurs who formed Halo Country LLC. The married couple had plans to obtain a Sonic franchise, but Sonic advised them to buy Halo Burger and convert them into Sonic locations. But the pair, who enjoyed going to Halo Burger while traveling north, preferred to revive the historic local-to-Flint brand.

They closed five underperforming locations, improved the quality of ingredients, lowered prices and raised employee pay. They also spent $2.5 million on restaurant renovations and computer upgrades. The new owners also provided assistance to Flint residents in reaction to the Flint water crisis, which happened as they were acquiring the Halo Burger chain, and insisted on using Michigan vendors for their food and supplies.

The 2020 COVID-19 pandemic did put a crimp on their operations due to having to close their dining areas and concentrate on service from their drive-through windows. The related labor shortage led to the permanent closing of the location on Flint's east side on Court Street near Center Road, and the former Kewpee flagship downtown location in the old Vernor's outlet temporarily closed. But while it was closed, the kitchen, dining areas and restrooms were updated, and it reopened on August 16, 2021.

As of this writing, Halo Burger has seven locations in the Flint area as far north as Birch Run and as far south as Fenton. These include the flagship downtown Flint location, which was formerly Kewpee Hamburgs. Halo Burger, like the surviving Kewpee locations in Lansing, Lima and Racine, makes burgers with fresh, never frozen beef.

4

THE KEWPEE LOCATIONS STILL IN OPERATION IN THE ORDER THAT THEY WERE FOUNDED

Kewpee of Lansing / East Lansing, Michigan

The Original Lansing Kewpee Hotel

The oldest-surviving Kewpee licensee is in Michigan's capital city, Lansing. Besides being Michigan's capital, Lansing is also a major automotive center. Ransom Olds started two notable automotive brands that no longer exist: Oldsmobile, which became a General Motors subsidiary, and REO, which survived into the 1970s. The Lansing Kewpee Hotel opened on November 1, 1924, at 115 West Shiawassee Street in the northern part of downtown. Lansing Kewpee founder Charles Wright sold it shortly afterward to William Bowlin and his wife, Gladys. They aligned themselves with Kewpee founder Sam Blair to develop the Lansing Kewpee Hotel location noted for the restaurant's white exterior. The franchise agreement Bowlin had with Blair involved only the napkins and the burger wrappers bearing the Kewpee trademarks.

Early on, the Olive Burgers were noted for their original olive sauce created by Gladys, which is still used by the Lansing Kewpee today. With the repeal of Prohibition in 1933, Bowlin opened the Kewpee Beer Store next door to the Kewpee Hotel the following year. It lasted only a year, and the Kewpee Hotel restaurant absorbed the beer store's space. In the 1920s and 1930s, Kewpee sponsored amateur baseball teams. The eatery started

Original Kewpee Hamburgs of Lansing, Michigan location on Shiawassee Street. Elmer Smith and his daughter Marjorie Harrison are in the photo. *Courtesy of Forest Parke Library & Archives, Capital Area District Libraries and Bill Harrison.*

Interior of original Lansing Kewpee on Shiawassee Street. *Vintage photo by James Tepin, courtesy of Karen Tepin-Winsinski.*

operating twenty-four hours a day in 1938. Located near Lansing Central High School, whose location became Lansing Community College in 1957, it became a popular hangout spot for students.

After William Bowlin died on January 23, 1940, at the young age of forty-five after a long illness, Gladys ran the restaurant for six years before turning it over to her son from her first marriage, Russell Weston.

While the 1950s brought new competition from drive-in restaurants that were springing up in Lansing's suburbs, most of Kewpee's old customers came back after about a year. The location across from Lansing Community College continued to be a major Lansing hangout spot.

But in 1966, urban renewal and Lansing Community College's growing pains led the City of Lansing to condemn the landmark hamburger haven. Bowlin and Weston fought the condemnation, and it remained in litigation even after the landmark restaurant was forced to close on April 6, 1973, and was torn down four days later. It wasn't until 1976 that the Michigan Court of Appeals gave its final ruling regarding compensation given of $184,127. The result was a mixed blessing for the Lansing Kewpee. While Kewpee won the case, it lost about five years' worth of interest to Weston and other defendants in the case.

While Bowlin and Weston were battling the condemnation of their restaurant, a basketball team Kewpee sponsored in 1973 won the Class A Michigan Recreation and Park Association championship game, which was held nearby in Flint at Northwestern High School. The Kewpee team advanced to the national regional tournament and finished second, losing to the team representing Minnesota in Elgin, Illinois, at Elgin Community College. That team was nominated for inclusion in the Greater Lansing Sports Hall of Fame.

Weston owned property at the corner of East Saginaw Street and North Grand Avenue just north of the old location, but the city zoning board, under pressure from the location's commercial neighbors, turned down his request to move Kewpee to that location. But Kewpee in Lansing was not going away.

KEWPEE IN EAST LANSING

In 1929, Bowlin opened Kewpee No. 2 in East Lansing at 325 East Grand River Avenue across from the campus of what is now Michigan State University. Like many Kewpee locations when they first opened, it was a simple hamburger stand measuring twenty feet by twenty feet. In 1933, Bowlin sold the East Lansing location to Severin Jean, who also owned Jean's Cocktail Lounge in downtown Lansing.

In 1939, Jean expanded his Kewpee stand to a much larger cafeteria, calling it Jean's Cafeteria while still offering "Kewpee Hamburgs." While the neon sign above the entrance read "Jean's Cafeteria," the rest of the sign on the façade stated it offered dinners, steaks and chops as well as Kewpee Hamburgs. The sign mounted from the roof facing Grand River read only "Kewpee Hamburgs Cafeteria" and stated the restaurant was air conditioned. There was also a small Coca-Cola sign above it.

The interior of the new cafeteria was impressive. The building measured 48 feet wide and 129 feet deep. The main dining area seated 300, and the banquet room, called the Blue Room, seated 120. It was open twenty-four hours a day and quickly became a popular hangout spot for Michigan State students.

In 1947, Jean retired from the food business and sold Jean's Cafeteria to a group headed by Ralph Monk, who renamed the business Ralph's Kewpee Cafeteria. At the time of the sale, daily sales tallied several hundred dollars, compared to 1933, when Jean bought the East Lansing Kewpee, when it took in about $15 daily. In 1950, Monk sold Ralph's Cafeteria to Marie Longson, who kept the Ralph's name and continued to offer Kewpee hamburgers.

Vintage Jean's Cafeteria/Kewpee Hamburgs in East Lansing across from the Michigan State campus. *Courtesy of Forest Parke Library & Archives, Capital Area District Libraries.*

In 1953, illness forced Longson to sell her Kewpee Cafeteria. According to a classified ad she placed in the *Chicago Tribune*, it was grossing $200,000 annually, and she was offering it for $50,000. Nicholas Tessaris acquired Ralph's Kewpee and also kept the name. It continued to be a hangout for Michigan State students who were tired of dorm food and were attracted to the reasonable prices Ralph's offered. By the 1960s, the business hours were 6:00 a.m. to midnight.

In 1965, Nicholas Tessaris turned over control of the restaurant to his son Spiro. He dropped the Kewpee affiliation and changed the name of the restaurant to Spiro's Cafeteria. Its slogan was "a meal for the price of a sandwich." During the turbulent '60s, Spiro's Cafeteria was also a gathering place for student events such as poetry readings. One event in May 1966 there called "Culture-Fest" attracted 150 students for an evening of poetry, spoken word performances and folk and jazz music. A student activist organization called Committee for Student Rights made Spiro's a headquarters of sorts. At that time, students still called Spiro's "Kewpee's," and its patrons were nicknamed "Kewpeeites." But in 1968, a larger three-story Jacobson's department store was announced for that site, forcing Spiro's Cafeteria to close. It, along with an adjacent gas station, was torn down and served as a temporary parking lot until the store was built and opened in 1970. That building is now the City Center Building.

Nicholas Tessaris died in 1981 at age eighty-seven. Spiro Tessaris, who became a successful real estate agent following the cafeteria's closing, died in 2011 at age eighty-one.

Kewpee Returns to Lansing

The year is 1976. It had been nearly three years since the Lansing Kewpee was forced to close its original location on Shiawassee Street in the name of progress. The Michigan Court of Appeals had ruled that Ingham County Circuit Court judge Donald L. Reisig, while he was correct in finding the Kewpee "a unique hamburger shop" and a "downtown institution…ideally located for its business," he should have calculated a $184,127 condemnation award from the date of possession by city authorities, not from the date they first filed against the restaurant. That meant, as stated already, that Weston and several other defendants in the case lost five years' worth of interest.

But now Weston was ready to reopen Kewpee. But not downtown yet. He did have plans to convert a vacant storefront that was previously the Harryman shoe store in the 100 block of South Washington, which was

A 1976 ad for Weston's Kewpee on South Pennsylvania Avenue. *Courtesy of Timothy Bowman.*

considered to be Lansing's first brick store building, into a walk-in restaurant. But he was not yet ready to work on it. What he did do was to rent an old fast-food restaurant in Lansing's south side at 5559 South Pennsylvania Avenue and open Weston's Kewpee Sandwich Shoppe.

In 1979, Russell's son Gary was ready to open the downtown location at 118 South Washington. Gary began working at the original Shiawassee Street location at age ten. He is a 1968 graduate of Michigan State, having majored in hotel and restaurant management. In renovating the downtown location, the walls were stripped to the original brick, and old barnwood was purchased with black walnut and white oak beams, which were installed using mortise joints and locks without nails to give the restaurant an old-fashioned look. Inside, it is decorated with Kewpee memorabilia, including the old signs from the Shiawassee Street location.

First generation co-owner Gladys Bowlin, a native of Hamilton, Ontario, who immigrated with her first husband, Harry Weston, to Michigan in 1920, lived to the ripe old age of ninety-eight, passing away on March 19, 1998.

In 1992, the south side location moved to a larger restaurant space at 6525 South Pennsylvania. The new location had double the space of the old location and allowed staffing to increase from forty-five to sixty. In 2005, that location was sold and became Zeus' Coney Island.

Back to the single location in downtown Lansing: Gary Weston's daughter Autumn started working for her father when she was a kid. She had always wanted to work with her dad, and in 2008, her dad handed the reins of the landmark restaurant to her, putting Weston's Kewpee restaurant in the fourth generation of family management.

The 2020 COVID pandemic was Weston's Kewpee's biggest challenge since the forced closing of its original location. Forced to rely on curbside takeout service until the dining area was allowed to open again, their loyal customers as well as the Lansing community rallied in their support for the nearly century-old dining establishment to keep Kewpee not only open and thriving but also continuing to provide the Lansing area with its famous burgers and other menu items for another century. In fact, the trademark Olive Burger was entered in Miami Beach, Florida's South Beach Wine & Food Festival's Burger Bash and won the judges' best burger award in 2020. It won Weston's Kewpee a trophy and $2,500.

Along with the loyalty of customers, there is loyalty among the Weston's Kewpee staff. The best example is with Tammie Bunker, who is a forty-year employee of the landmark restaurant, hired by Gary Weston straight from high school after her graduation. She serves as a mentor to younger Kewpee employees and enlivens both staff and customers with her lively and giggly personality. About her job, she said, "I love my customers, and the Westons are family." Tammie even served as a sort-of teacher to Autumn before the younger Weston took over managing the restaurant. Autumn stated, "She's not an owner, but she could be because of how much she cares."

During the summer and fall of 2022, the front façade of Weston's Kewpee was remodeled. The entrance received a new door, and an additional door was installed, which allowed the upstairs' occupant of the building to enter from outside. On Halloween 2022, Weston's Kewpee Burger's new sign featuring the classic Kewpie doll mascot was unveiled.

After the second-generation owner of Weston's Kewpee Burger, Russell Weston, died on August 11, 2017, Douglas P. Emerson wrote the following poem as a tribute to him. A framed copy of this poem is on display in Weston's Kewpee's dining area:

Above: Interior of Weston's Kewpee with trophy won in Miami, Florida, in foreground. *Author photo*.

Right: Weston's Kewpee in Lansing, Michigan, on South Washington Square today. *Author photo*.

Everyday, rain or shine, he was there
Kewpee's was his place
Greeting folks as they arrive
Kind words and a smile on his face

Shiawassee St. was his first location
One of the first drive-up's in the land
Up the alley and give your order
Then a bag placed in your hand

Knotty pine walls with a juke box in the back
It could have been the set of a TV show
An Olive Burger or one with everything
That's all one needed to know

Every bite brings back a memory
It is still the same food today
Hamburg, pickle on top makes your heart go flippity flop
What more can anyone say

Russell Weston he was the man
Known, loved and respected by all
Heaven will now have Kewpee burgers
Something to remember when we get the call

KEWPEE IN RACINE, WISCONSIN

In 1926, Dick Sanford opened a Kewpee Hamburgs stand in Racine, Wisconsin, at 520 Wisconsin Street. Located along Lake Michigan between Milwaukee and Chicago, Racine is noted for its varied industries, most notably tractor manufacturing, garbage disposals and household products. Among the staff at this Kewpee location was a young man named Allen Durkee who went by the nickname Speck. In 1930, Sanford sold the hamburger stand to Walter Block, who retained Durkee as an employee.

In 1939, Block moved the hamburger stand from the front of the lot to the back of the lot, allowing for the construction of a full-size restaurant with the sign on the front saying "Kewpee Lunch" with the Kewpie doll mascot above it. The old stand was torn down upon completion of the restaurant.

Original Kewpee Lunch in Racine, Wisconsin, 1940s. *Courtesy of Trudy Kristopeit.*

Block died in 1957. Speck and his wife, Emily Durkee, bought the restaurant from Block's estate. In 1962, the City of Racine built a parking structure above the restaurant. It stayed open during construction.

In 1963, Speck died. His widow asked her brother Richard Kristopeit, who had worked at the restaurant part time since high school, to manage it. He bought the restaurant from his sister in 1968.

In 1972, Richard sold it to his two sons, David and Rick. David Kristopeit started working at age fourteen, and Rick followed his brother the following year after he turned fourteen. David bought out Rick's share in 1992. Dave's wife, Trudy, along with their children Mike, Katie and Joshua joined in working at the Kewpee, making the establishment a family affair. They included Trudy's brother Richard Buehrens, who began working there in 1976.

In 1995, it was determined that the parking ramp above the Kewpee had become unsafe and needed to be demolished. This time, the Kewpee Lunch location below it was doomed, as engineers determined that they could not tear down the ramp while leaving the Kewpee intact.

The City of Racine used eminent domain to acquire the Kewpee location. But another downtown Racine location to move Kewpee to was not to be found. So after the location closed on May 31, 1997, the parking ramp and Kewpee were torn down during June and July. David Kristopeit bought the resulting vacant lot back from the city in order to build a replacement Kewpee restaurant.

During construction of the new Kewpee, the staff was kept busy by catering a picnic for employees of Racine's major employer, the household products company S.C. Johnson, on August 2, 1997. They served 4,500 hamburgers, which took five chefs over four hours to cook 720 pounds of ground beef.

The new Kewpee on the site of the old one opened on November 22, 1997. It retained the art deco look of the old restaurant with a seating capacity of forty-eight compared to thirty-six at the old restaurant with parking for fifteen cars. It was also handicap accessible. Inside, there is a large display case holding an amazing collection of Kewpie dolls.

In 2003, David sold the restaurant to longtime manager and brother-in-law Buehrens, who ran it along with his wife, Mary, and son Andrew. Andrew began working part time there at age fourteen and was appointed by his father as the full-time manager of Kewpee in 2018.

The Kewpee in Racine does not have a drive-through window. So when the COVID pandemic broke out in March 2020 and Wisconsin forced nonessential businesses to close, Kewpee had to close for a couple of months. It was allowed to reopen at the end of May with the seating capacity limited to fifteen and only for patrons to wait for takeout orders. The closed seating areas were marked off. The dining area was allowed to

Kewpee restaurant in Racine, Wisconsin today, built on the site of the original Kewpee Lunch. *Courtesy of Joel Rash.*

Interior of the Kewpee restaurant in Racine, Wisconsin. *Courtesy of Joel Rash.*

fully reopen in January 2021 when Racine allowed for 50 percent capacity in restaurants.

The Kewpee in downtown Racine managed to survive the pandemic and continues to provide Racine with award-winning hamburgers. Kewpee won *Racine Journal Times* Best Burger surveys multiple times, and in 2021, the paper gave Kewpee awards for Best Burger and Best Lunch. The business also won the Best Burger award in 2022. Sadly, David Kristopeit, who helped the author in writing this book, died on January 19, 2023, at age seventy-three. As already mentioned, this book is dedicated to his memory.

THE KEWPEE RESTAURANTS IN LIMA, OHIO

In 1928, a young couple from Battle Creek, Michigan, named Hoyt (nicknamed "Stub" or "Stubby") and June Wilson were inspired by the Kewpee Hotel hamburger stands in Michigan to move to Lima, Ohio, to establish their own Kewpee Hotel location downtown. Lima is located in northwestern Ohio, and the state's oil industry began there. When the Wilsons were running out of money to build their hamburger stand, they borrowed from Stub's father in Alma, Michigan, to install a water line. Stub's dad replied at that time that Stub might as well just dig a hole and bury the

A 1929 photo of the Original Kewpee Hotel stand in Lima after the stand was fully enclosed. *Courtesy of Kewpee Inc.*

money, as he had those thoughts about his son's new enterprise. The money was paid back with generous interest.

That original stand had a covered walk-up window on one side of the building and a drive-up window on the other side. There was also a counter with wooden stools. Hours were originally 8:30 a.m. to 2:00 p.m. Hamburgers were five cents and bottled beer was ten cents. After the Wilsons realized they were catering to a family clientele, the beer, introduced in 1930 when Ohio American Legionnaires held their convention in Lima, did not last long. The menu was simple, with hamburgers, cola, root beer, milkshakes, pie and coffee. A year later, the covered walk-up area was completely enclosed with a front door and side windows.

Wishing to add a second restaurant in Findlay, Ohio, Stub Wilson realized that someone else opened a Kewpee Hotel restaurant there. So in 1936, he opened Wilson's Sandwich Stop, which is still in operation today.

The small Lima restaurant was successful, so in 1939, the Wilsons decided to build a new, larger Kewpee Hotel restaurant on the same site. Kewpee trademark owner Edwin Adams wanted to open a location in Utica, New York. Both locations were built using similar designs created by the Davidson Enamel Products Company in Lima featuring a porcelain/enamel finish that was becoming popular with gasoline stations. The new restaurant had central air conditioning, one of the first buildings in Lima to have central air, and an expanded menu that included frosted malts. It also added curb service, replacing the drive-up window. This allowed patrons to eat in their cars. Curb service was pioneered by root beer stands such as A&W but was a new feature for hamburger shops. Later on, curb service was discontinued, and the Kewpee went back to the drive-up window.

To allow for drive-up window service in Kewpee's narrow parking area along the side of the restaurant, a turntable was installed on the back of the lot, allowing for cars to be turned around to access the drive-through window. The turntable was a huge hit for the kids. It was operated

Flagship Kewpee in Lima, Ohio, after it was completed in 1939. *Courtesy of Kewpee Inc.*

The Kewpee location servicing Lima's west side. *Courtesy of Kewpee Inc.*

from the back of the lot. In 1955, that turntable was replaced by one that was operated from inside the restaurant. The sixteen-foot-diameter turntable was supplied by the Macton Machinery Company of Stamford, Connecticut.

In 1957, Harrison Shutt began working at the restaurant. Shortly afterward, an adjacent apartment building was sold and torn down, allowing Kewpee to expand its parking area and eliminating the need for the turntable.

In 1967, Stub Wilson died, and June took control. In 1970, Shutt was appointed as general manager. In 1972, he opened a second Kewpee location in Lima's west side on Allentown Road. Popular demand led to the addition of French fries to the menu in 1975. An addition to the downtown location had to be built to accommodate the fryers.

In 1977, the old James G. Mackenzie mansion behind the Allentown Road location was purchased and leased to the operator of a senior center for about a year. The following year, after losing access to the borrowed downtown parking lot, the adjacent Kern Building was sold and razed to expand the narrow parking lot. At the same time, the mansion behind the Allentown Road location was torn down.

June Wilson died in 1979, and Shutt took over the Lima Kewpee locations. Around 1980, a third location was added, serving the east side of Lima

Left: Kewpie statue in front of original Kewpee Hotel burger wrapper design at the Kewpee of Lima east side location on Bellefontaine Avenue. *Author photo. © Kewpee Inc.*

Below: The Kewpee location serving Lima's east side. *Author photo.*

on Bellefontaine Avenue. This location not only includes a large Kewpie statue in the dining area, but it also has an exhibit that gives a visual history of Kewpee in Lima. In 1985, Kewpee of Lima acquired the trademarks, copyrights and federal registrations for Kewpee hamburgers. In 1986, drive-through service was added to the Allentown Road location.

Kewpee of Lima helps out Lima-area residents with charitable work such as sponsoring various events in the city. This includes Kewpee's sponsorship of events in the Allen County Fair, the annual Kewpee High School Art Invitational at ArtSpace/Lima, the Kewpee/Lima YMCA Triathlon/Duathlon, the Ohio Northern University's Holiday Spectacular and Coach Q's Kewpee Holiday Classic Showcase at Lima Senior High School, among others the business sponsors or cosponsors. Kewpee also helped raise funds over the years for Lima Central Catholic High School by the school selling coupons good for free food when redeemed. Kewpee coupons were also sold by the Lima Senior High School Athletic Department to benefit the Lima City Schools Athletic Department.

Today, Kewpee of Lima is operated by Harrison Shutt and his son Scott. They continue to license the rights to operate Kewpee restaurants in Lansing, Michigan, and Racine, Wisconsin.

The landmark downtown Kewpee location was mentioned in a book by Donna Hanover titled *My Boyfriend's Back: True Stories of Rediscovering Love with Long-Lost Sweethearts*. The local hangout spot was name checked in a piece in that book titled "Heather and Scott: There's Only So Much to Celebrity, and Then You Go Home."

5

KEWPEE INSPIRED WENDY'S

Rex David Thomas, better known as Dave Thomas, had a rough childhood. Born in Atlantic City, New Jersey, to an unmarried couple, he was adopted as a baby by Rex and Auleva Thomas of Kalamazoo, Michigan. But Auleva died when he was five, forcing his adoptive father to move around the country searching for work. During the summer months, he was left in the care of his grandmother in Kalamazoo. He picked up the work ethic that would serve him in adulthood from his grandmother. In Kalamazoo, he lived near the Kewpee location on East South Street near Burdick Street. He loved eating at that Kewpee restaurant. His grandmother taught him the value of work.

For a time, he and his father lived in a rooming house in Detroit that had no kitchen. So they ate in restaurants. Dave appreciated watching the other patrons enjoy themselves while eating. So he vowed at age eight that he would own his own restaurant. At age twelve, lying about his age, he was hired as a counter man at the Regas Restaurant in Knoxville, Tennessee. There, owners Frank and George Regas treated employees like family, and Thomas found in the Regas brothers his first mentors. But his father found another job in Fort Wayne, Indiana, and Dave was forced to quit, but he left his dream job on good terms with the Regas brothers.

In Fort Wayne, again lying about his age at fifteen, he found work at the Hobby House restaurant as a busboy. His hard work led him to be promoted to working at the soda fountain four weeks later. He made quite an impression with Hobby House owner Phil Clauss, and Dave was surprised that Clauss

The Kewpee Hotel in Kalamazoo, Michigan where Wendy's founder Dave Thomas recalled dining as a child. *Courtesy of Kalamazoo Public Library.*

was sweeping floor and busing dishes. So Clauss became another mentor to Dave as he aspired to learn every aspect of the restaurant business. But when his father had to move again, Dave stayed behind in Fort Wayne to continue working at the Hobby House. He dropped out of school and lived at the nearby YMCA. Phil Clauss suggested it, and Dave agreed to live with Clauss's sister's family.

In 1950, the Korean War broke out, and at age eighteen, Dave Thomas enlisted in the army to avoid the draft, aspiring to serve as a cook. He spent eight weeks at the Cook and Baker's School. He was stationed in Frankfurt, Germany, as a mess sergeant and served for over two years.

After Thomas was discharged in October 1953, he returned to the Hobby House and met his future wife, Lorraine. He was promoted to assistant manager of the co-owned Hobby Ranch House. In 1956, Colonel Harland Sanders stopped at Hobby House to pitch that the restaurant offer his unique method of frying chicken. That was the start of Dave Thomas's association with Kentucky Fried Chicken. The deal was the restaurant would buy Sanders's secret spices and some pressure cookers. He would get a five-cent royalty for every chicken sold.

While Thomas had his doubts about the colonel's deal with Phil Clauss, once he tasted the chicken, he was sold. So were the customers at the Hobby House, as the Kentucky Fried Chicken sales were very strong. Customer input led the Hobby House to offer takeout orders for the chicken. As part of the push for takeout orders, Thomas invented the cardboard bucket to put the fried chicken pieces in. As the KFC takeout operations took off, Thomas created the red and white façade appearance for the Kentucky Fried Chicken locations and introduced the large revolving bucket sign bearing Colonel Sanders's face.

Clauss also had a financial interest in KFC operations in Columbus, Ohio. But those locations were losing money. So Clauss assigned Thomas to move to Columbus to turn around those locations in 1961. Thomas simplified the menu to just chicken, mashed potatoes, gravy and a roll. The Hobby Ranch House was renamed Kentucky Fried Chicken. Thomas was successful in turning those KFC restaurants around.

In 1964, Colonel Sanders sold KFC to a group of investors led by Sanders's lawyer and future Kentucky governor John Y. Brown and entrepreneur Jack C. Massey. Thomas's success in turning around the Ohio KFC franchises got their attention. Brown and Massey appointed Thomas as regional manager of all KFC locations east of the Mississippi. Meanwhile, Thomas began investing in National Diversified, which owned restaurants that did not directly compete with KFC. But Brown and Massey thought differently, and the fallout as well as a KFC stock deal gone bad led to Thomas quitting KFC in 1968. He sued regarding the bad stock deal and won his case.

For about a year, he had a hand in developing National Diversified's then new Arthur Treacher's Fish & Chips restaurants while still dreaming of his own hamburger restaurant. Here is a quote from Thomas's book *Dave's Way*:

> *Hamburgers were always my favorite food, and I just felt that I understood them better than anybody. Back at the Hobby Ranch House, Dick Clauss—Phil's son—and I looked at a lot of hamburger places. We'd see a store or stand or a restaurant that was a little different, and we would go in and take a look at it. We'd have a hamburger and ask a lot of questions. Phil personally knew a man in Lima, Ohio, Stubby Wilson, who had a great hamburger operation. It was called the Kewpee Hamburger Stand, and I learned a lot from it. They made hamburgers fresh off the grill and sold them as fast as they could get them out. Stubby bought beef rounds and ground his own hamburger. He was a great believer in fresh merchandise and fresh products. Stubby's ideas on hamburgers stuck in the back of my mind.*

A friend of Thomas's, car dealer Len Immke, owned a former car dealership building in Columbus, Ohio, of which he was using the service area to prep new Buicks for his nearby dealership. But the old showroom, which was previously occupied by a restaurant, was vacant. So Immke encouraged Thomas to take over that space for the first Wendy's Old Fashioned Hamburger restaurant, which served square hamburgers just like Kewpee in Lima and was named after one of Thomas's daughters. It opened on November 15, 1969. That was the start of Wendy's, which grew with the help of Massey, who left Kentucky Fried Chicken in 1970. Massey opened several Wendy's franchises. Wendy's now has over six thousand locations in North America, partially inspired by Kewpee.

The original Wendy's restaurant at 257 East Broad Street in Columbus has been renovated and now houses the Catholic Foundation. An Ohio Historical Marker for the "Site of First Wendy's Restaurant" was installed in 2007 by Wendy's International and the Ohio Historical Society.

6

KEWPEE'S PLACE IN HAMBURGER RESTAURANT HISTORY

As already mentioned, Kewpee is the second-oldest hamburger chain in the United States, with White Castle (founded in 1921) being the oldest. White Castle's success spawned numerous imitators with similar names, the most notable and blatant being White Tower, which led to lawsuits by White Castle. The original won, forcing White Tower to pay fees to White Castle and redesign its restaurants to look less like White Castle wannabes. Ironically, there is only one White Tower remaining, located in Toledo, Ohio, where Kewpee was based for decades. That restaurant was forced to close due to a fire in April 2022, but as of March 2023 it was still closed.

Like Kewpee, White Castle began in the Midwest. But unlike Kewpee, White Castle avoided licensing its restaurants, and all restaurants are company owned. This practice of only opening its own restaurants meant a slow growth, and White Castle's 375 or so locations today are mainly concentrated in the northeastern United States with a handful of locations in other regions. White Castle controls its supply distribution, which limits the brand's ability to make the chain truly national. But its flagship sliders are nationally available in the frozen food section of supermarkets.

There are other closely held hamburger chains that are regional and have a loyal customer base. They include Whataburger in the southeastern United States but concentrated more in Texas and In-N-Out Burger in the southwestern United States but concentrated more in California.

The White Castle location in Flint. *Author photo.*

Whataburger's flagship hamburger of that name is noted for its oversized bun to accommodate the large burger patty and may have inspired Burger King's flagship burger, the Whopper.

The number of White Castle locations are a small fraction compared to the national burger chains such as McDonald's, Burger King and Kewpee-influenced Wendy's. But there were once other large burger chains. But a combination of factors led to their decline. Burger Chef was once second only to McDonald's in the number of locations. It was absorbed into another hamburger chain, Hardee's. The owner of another hamburger chain in the Northeast, Carroll's, decided to switch to operating Burger King restaurants in the 1970s. While the major fast-food hamburger chains, such as McDonald's (under CEO Ray Kroc), put their franchisees on short leashes, insisting on standardizing the menus and making sure the food was the same at every location, Kewpee under Samuel Blair and then Edwin Adams gave Kewpee licensees no leashes, so the hamburgers at Kewpee licensees in different cities were not always the same.

Other burger chains tried to expand outside their established regions but could not quite make it as national brands. But Jack in the Box, a western United States chain with isolated locations elsewhere, ranks fifth in order of locations behind McDonald's followed by Burger King, Wendy's and Sonic. Sonic is noted for being strictly a drive-in restaurant, harkening back to when drive-in restaurants were popular decades ago.

There are national chains with regional differences, as when one regional fast-food chain buys another regional fast-food chain. Carl's Jr., based in the western United States, owns Hardee's in the East. Checkers, based in the South, and Rally's, based in the North, merged and are still operating under both names. Checkers and Rally's are noted because most of their locations are drive-through only.

The proliferation of the larger franchise hamburger restaurants with diversified menus made it more difficult for the smaller burger places to compete. The smaller chains made three choices, two of which are already mentioned. Switch to being a franchisee of a larger burger chain, sell to another burger chain that would convert the locations to the new name or simply close up shop. That does not include locations forced to close due to eminent domain such as the original Kewpee Hotel location in Lansing, Michigan.

As for Kewpee, the *Muncie Evening Press* reported in 1929 when the Kewpee location there opened. Rose O'Neill, who created the Kewpie doll that became Kewpee's mascot, allowed for the use of her creation with the altered spelling of the name as the name of the restaurant, and she supervised the design of the Kewpie doll on the signs for the hamburger stands and restaurants. Regarding the fate of the Kewpee chain with the four hundred or so boasted locations but with only forty-one communities found with Kewpee locations, several factors led to Kewpee's decline through the years. There were the effects of the Great Depression, World War II–era meat shortages, locations going independent of the Kewpee fold for various reasons or simply the inability to compete with the larger fast-food restaurants. Eminent domain forced closing is another reason, as happened with the original Kewpee Hotel location in Lansing, Michigan. Ironically, Halo Burger, which began as the very first Kewpee location, broke away from Kewpee in 1967 and still has a location in downtown Flint. It has more locations, with seven in and around its home base of Flint, compared to Kewpee, with five locations total in Lima, Ohio; Lansing, Michigan; and Racine, Wisconsin.

7

BEYOND BURGERS

Today, we consider burgers and fries going hand in hand at any fast-food hamburger restaurant. But several Kewpee locations did not offer fries originally. The very first Kewpee location in Flint that evolved into Halo Burger did not offer French fries until 1950. The landmark Kewpee restaurant in Lima, as mentioned previously, did not offer fries until 1975.

The photo of the original Kewpee Hotel stand in Flint indicated that it offered Stroh's beer back then. The Kewpee Hotel stand in Lima also offered beer in the 1930s. Other Kewpee locations that offered beer included locations in the Michigan cities of Benton Harbor, Lansing (in the adjacent co-owned beer store) and Niles.

Early on, frosted malteds were offered at Kewpee locations. That was the case when the oldest-surviving Kewpee restaurant opened in Lima in 1939; malts served in a frosted soda glass proved to be popular there. The original sign there proclaimed that the Kewpee offered them.

Today, the Kewpee locations in Lima, along with their burger offerings, include the following sandwiches: fish (added in 2004), cold cheese and vegetable. Their sides include fries, chili, fresh-baked pie, frosted malteds and soft frozen yogurt. The breakfast menu includes breakfast sandwiches, hash browns, donuts, sweet rolls and orange juice.

On display at Weston's Kewpee in Lansing are a pair of old drive-through menu boards from the original location on Shiawassee Street. Along with the burger offerings, it also offered back then the following sandwiches: ham, ham and cheese, grilled cheese, tuna and fish. It also offered hot dogs, French

This page, top: A 1950 Kewpee Hotel Flint ad announcing they now offer French fries. *Courtesy of Wendy All.*

This page, bottom: Two drive-through menu boards from the long-gone original Kewpee location in Lansing, Michigan. *Author photos.*

Opposite: Recent menu from Weston's Kewpee in Lansing. *Courtesy of Weston's Kewpee and Timothy Bowman.*

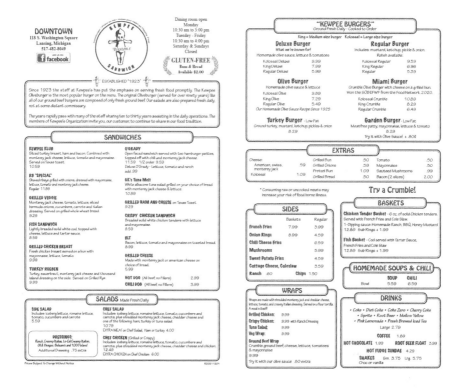

fries, malts, hot fudge, sundaes and shrimp. The second old drive-through menu board added a fish dinner and onion rings.

As with many other fast-food restaurants through the years, the Lansing Kewpee's menu offerings became much larger. Add the following sandwiches—roast beef, grilled veggie, grilled chicken breast, turkey Reuben, crispy chicken and BLT. It also offers salads.

The Lansing Kewpee's sides added chili cheese fries, mushrooms, sweet potato fries, cottage cheese, coleslaw and chips. It also offers the following wraps: grilled chicken, crispy chicken, tuna salad, veggie and ground beef. It sells chicken and fish baskets along with homemade shops and chili.

Kewpee in Racine added to its burger menu fishburgers (with or without cheese), chicken filet, toasted cheese, cheese sandwich, French fries, potato chips and chili.

Halo Burger in the Flint area, which was the original Kewpee until 1967, along with its various burger offerings, includes in the latest menu chicken sandwiches, chicken strips and Flint-style Coney Island hot dogs. Along with milkshakes, it offers a Boston Cooler made with Vernors ginger ale and vanilla ice cream, fried apple pie, chocolate chip cookies and bumpy cake.

Along with fries, it offers tater tots, cheese curds, onion rings, dino nuggets, "Halopeños," Coney cheese fries and Coney cheese tots. During the Lenten season, between the Christian observances of Ash Wednesday and Easter, Halo sells fish sandwiches.

Vintage ads for Kewpee locations that no longer exist advertised a few non-burger items. During the Lenten season, the Kewpee in Battle Creek offered vegetable and egg sandwiches in 1929. That same year, the Kewpee in St. Joseph, Michigan, offered hot dogs. In 1955, the Kewpee Hotel in Benton Harbor, Michigan included on its menu chicken, fish, shrimp, malteds and French fries. In a 1949 Kewpee of Grand Rapids, Michigan ad, the restaurant advertised a vegetable sandwich, donuts, eclairs, pies, French fries, soups, chili and sundaes. When the Kewpee Hotel in Sandusky, Ohio, opened in 1939, it also offered chili, frosted malteds, pies, rolls and cereal. The Kewpee in South Bend, Indiana, also offered frosted malts. In a vintage coupon ad, Kewpee in Toledo plugged its chili, fries and frosteds. The Kewpee Lunch that was in Winona, Minnesota, also offered French fries along with batter-fried pike and chicken.

8

LOST KEWPEES

The book about the history of White Castle published in 1997 titled *Selling 'em by the Sack* claimed that there were more than four hundred Kewpee locations at the start of World War II. But the former Kewpee locations are mostly lost to time. Visits to libraries for city directories and internet searches using such services as archive.org and newspapers.com yielded only a handful of these claimed locations. A total of forty-four communities were found that had at least one Kewpee hamburger stand or restaurant. Of these communities, only twenty-six had sufficient information to have pieces of varying lengths written about them. Not included on the following pieces is the Kewpee cafeteria in East Lansing, Michigan, already mentioned in the earlier Kewpee of Lansing/East Lansing piece. Here are the lost Kewpees with the cities listed in alphabetical order.

KEWPEE IN AKRON, OHIO

Along with his flagship Kewpee Hotel location in Toledo, Ed Adams also owned the Kewpee Hotel location at 15 South High Street in Akron, Ohio, a city noted for its automotive tire industries. The building had previously housed a business called Sol's Drive It Yourself, and this Kewpee Hotel opened in 1933.

Early on, dice men and dealers from nearby gambling houses were patrons. Author Dick Stodghill mentioned this Kewpee Hotel in his paperback collection of short stories titled *Jack Eddy Stories*, vol. 2, in a piece called "A Policy For Murder." Later on, entertainers frequented the restaurant after performing in concerts and gigs. A few notable restaurateurs in Akron got their first jobs at that Kewpee. The staff would ground fifty to sixty pounds of fresh chuck every day for their burgers.

A frequent patron of the Akron Kewpee Hotel was Edward Lawrence, known as Eddie, who was employed beginning in 1949 across the street as a salesman for the Office Equipment Bureau. Because that business had four other employees named Eddie, he was given the nickname Larry after his surname. It was at this Kewpee that he got to know a supervising waitress named Mary, whom he married. After the Kewpee of Akron manager was reassigned to one of Adams's Toledo Kewpee locations, Lawrence was offered the job as the Akron Kewpee manager.

Lawrence got to know the restaurant's clientele, not the suburban solid citizens, but instead the dealers and dicemen from the gambling houses that were on East Market Street and on South Main Street. Nightclub performers also ate there. They included Scatman Crouthers and members of Charlie Barnet's or Woody Herman's band. Both performers and patrons from the nearby (but now demolished) Palace Theatre dined at Kewpee just a few doors away.

At this Kewpee's peak in the 1940s, it grossed as much as $250,000 a year and had twenty-eight employees.

In 1970, Eddie Lawrence purchased that Kewpee and changed its name to Larry's. In 1978, the Akron Art Museum purchased Larry's location, and the lease was not renewed. The following year, Larry's moved across the street at 16 South High Street to make way for a sculpture garden for the museum. In its later years, that location became a rough area.

When the nearby Hammel College moved from the area, business dropped off, and Larry's shortened its hours to weekdays from 7:00 a.m. to 5:00 p.m. Over the years, the Lawrences added soup, footlong hot dogs, chicken and other sandwiches.

Larry's closed in 1989. At the time of its closing, Mary and Ed Lawrence stated they never met a customer they didn't like. In thirty-five years of flipping burgers, nobody ever sent back a plate of food. Nor did the couple, who had dozens of policemen, attorneys, judges and—at times—prostitutes for customers, ever get robbed.

The restaurant's closing with the Lawrences' retirement brought them well-wishers. About a half-dozen staffers from the nearby Planned Parenthood office came singing with balloons. Longtime customers brought in gifts on the last day the hamburger shop was open. Ed stated, "I'm old, but I'm still emotional. I didn't want to cry."

The Larry's site was torn down to make way for a parking lot for the Akron Art Museum, and a large addition to the museum built on the former Larry's site opened in 2007 named the John S. and James L. Knight Building.

Mary Lawrence died in 2006 at age eighty-three. Eddie Lawrence died in 2012 at age ninety-one.

KEWPEE IN BATTLE CREEK, MICHIGAN

Willard H. Brown was part of a pioneering family in the Cereal City where cornflakes were invented by Will Kellogg, who founded the breakfast cereal company bearing his name. Will Kellogg invented cornflakes while working for his brother Dr. John Harvey Kellogg at his popular sanitarium as a health food. A patient there, Charles W. Post, was inspired by the diet offered at Dr. Kellogg's sanitarium to start his own cereal company. Today, both Kellogg's Cereal and Post Consumer Brands have extensive cereal manufacturing operations in Battle Creek.

Born in 1865 on his father's farm on the outskirts of Battle Creek, Brown moved to town in 1886 as an apprentice printer at the *Daily Moon* newspaper earning six dollars a week. He moved on, working for the American Express Company and drove a delivery wagon, becoming a familiar sight on Battle Creek streets. He then worked as a shipping clerk for the Advance Thresher Company, followed by running a livery stable. He returned to the *Moon* as circulation manager, working eight years there. Then he entered the bakery and restaurant business with a partner. Then he went into the business of buying and selling hay. By the early 1900s, he had his own grocery store and creamery with Battle Creek's first automotive delivery truck.

After selling the business, he moved to the southeastern United States to be a traveling salesman for the American Slicing Machine Company, covering territory in the Carolinas, Florida and Georgia. But feeling homesick, he returned to Battle Creek and worked for the distributor of Schlitz Beer. But the coming of Prohibition in 1920 led him to work for the U.S. Slicing Machine Company. In his travels, he discovered that hamburger stands had become a lucrative business.

So in 1928, he opened his first Kewpee Hotel hamburger stand at 31 West State Street in Battle Creek. Named Brown's Kewpee, at that stand, Brown developed his motto of "quality and service." A 1935 article about this Kewpee described the stand's operation beginning when a customer with four passengers drives into the lighted side street behind the Kewpee and honks the horn for service.

A white garbed waiter-cook promptly slides back a window of the "hotel" to take your order. When everyone has decided whether he prefers pickles and mustard or onions and catsup or some other combination from the row of jars at the Kewpee, the window is closed. Before the four of you have hardly had time to discuss the next tennis game, the window slides open again and out comes the food.

There is a sliding window in front of the hotel, too, and often pedestrians, noticing the neat, white lunch stand, remember it has been a long time since they had lunch and stop for a hamburg and bottle of pop.

Brown's Kewpee ground its own beef, purchased directly from the meatpacker, on the premises.

Brown's Kewpee became so successful that he moved to a larger location in 1936 at 59 West State Street. The new location was designed with sanitation in mind at one of the first all-porcelain-lined building of its type in Michigan and has porcelain baked bricks on the outside and a metal porcelain finish in the interior.

Both the interior and exterior smooth porcelain surfaces have all their cracks and joints sealed for easy cleaning. The terrazzo floor had curved corners that did not trap dirt. The atmosphere was a far cry from the usual greasy spoon environment of most hamburger places. The kitchen area had the latest equipment for efficient service, and the restaurant could easily hold fifty patrons.

The new restaurant was air conditioned in the summer and circulated fresh, warm air in the winter. A big suction fan above the cooking grills pulled the cooking heat and odors away from the dining areas. In the back was a walk-in refrigerator highly insulated and covered with cement. During the grand opening on July 8 and 9, 1936, a coupon was offered in the *Battle Creek Enquirer & Evening News* good for one sandwich and a drink. Six thousand sandwiches were served during the grand opening to children and adults. Brown estimated he would be using at least seventy-five head of cattle that year to make his hamburgers.

In 1942, Brown sold his Kewpee Hotel restaurant to employee John "Bud" Woolley, who had worked at Brown's Kewpee for ten years. The Brown's Kewpee name was retained. Later that year, Woolley was drafted into the

We Announce the Formal Opening of the New

BROWN'S KEWPEE

59 W. State St.
East of Elks Temple

*There Is No Other
Building of Its Kind
In Michigan to
Compare with It!*

Be Our Guests
Wednesday - Thursday

*Inspect Our New
Quarters Tomorrow.
Be Sure to Read the
Coupon Below!*

THE NEW BUILDING

Without a doubt, you'll agree that the new Brown's Kewpee is the finest building of its kind you'll find in any city in the State of Michigan.

Women in particular will admire the manner in which it can be kept spotlessly clean because it is all porcelain lined throughout. In fact, we have already overheard some women patrons express their desire for a similar wall and ceiling surface in their own kitchens.

Inside and out, we are able to keep our new building CLEAN, because the smooth porcelain surfaces are easily wiped off, and because all cracks and joints are sealed to prevent accumulation of dirt.

Terrazo floors with curved corners enable us to keep the floors free from dirt at all times.

In fact, our entire plan when constructing this building was to have one in which you could enjoy eating without being conscious of dirt, grease and other unpleasant features found in many places of this type.

SERVICE IS QUICK --- EFFICIENT

We are now able to serve fifty persons at one time—in booths, at tables, or at the counter. Individual orders are prepared in one minute or less—thus eliminating long waits. Faster cooking on our new grille enables us to serve you quickly and efficiently.

COOL, ODORLESS CIRCULATING AIR

Fresh air is cooled and circulated through our entire building by a large American Blower. This appliance also circulates fresh warm air in the winter time. Right now you will feel refreshed at all times when you step into Brown's Kewpee. You enjoy a much cooler temperature than outdoors, yet are not annoyed by a damp chilliness.

A big suction fan above our cooking grille takes all heat and cooking odors away from the kitchen and dining room. At no time are you aware that foods are being prepared within a few feet of you.

PERFECT REFRIGERATION

Not only do we buy the finest quality foods but we keep them properly in our new step-in refrigerator. This big box is lined with non-pariel cork board and again covered with cement. We can scrub this surface and keep the refrigerator odorless at all times.

BRING THE ENTIRE FAMILY

Children as well as adults can be brought to Brown's Kewpee with perfect assurance of being served high quality, well-prepared foods.

For your convenience we maintain two wash rooms. We know you'll like this additional feature.

*Be Sure to Visit Us
Tomorrow or Thursday
July 8th or 9th.*

Clip This Coupon
*We Invite Any Man, Woman or Child to be Our Guest
at Our Formal Opening*
THIS COUPON IS GOOD FOR
One Sandwich and a Drink
If Presented Between 10:00 A. M. and 5:00 P. M.
Wednesday or Thursday—July 8th or 9th
— PLEASE FILL IN BELOW —

Name .... Address ....

*Tell Your Friends About
The New Brown's Kewpee
And How You Enjoy It!*

Vintage 1936 Grand Opening Ad for Brown's Kewpee Restaurant. *From the* Battle Creek Enquirer, *newspapers.com.*

army, and his assistant, his brother-in-law Melton Bradshaw, took over running the restaurant. While Woolley was serving, Brown made numerous visits to his old restaurant, offering his advice and services and acting as sort of a guardian angel over the business for its soldier-owner. Brown died two years later at age seventy-eight.

Woolley apparently had a hobby of drawing panel cartoons, which appeared in a series of ads placed in the *Battle Creek Enquirer* in 1951–52. The cartoon captions included:

- "Come on! How can you be interested in fur coats, when we're on our way to lunch at BROWN's KEWPEE HAMBURGERS."
- "I think your prospective son-in-law has excellent taste, J.B....I see him eating regularly at BROWN'S KEWPEE."
- (in looking at suggestion box entries): "This one suggests that the management take all the employees out to BROWN'S KEWPEE for a couple of those delicious hamburgers."
- "I'm on a strict diet—Doctor's orders! But after tomorrow he says I can eat again—I'm going to BROWN'S for a Kewpee and fine dessert."
- "Miss Smith, take a farewell note. This company is transferring me to another district, and I can't bear the thought of leaving those wonderful Kewpees at BROWN'S KEWPEE HAMBURGERS!" (note the cartoon shows the executive on a ledge outside the high-rise office window)
- "Is he an educated bird? Why, lady, he only speaks to people who he is SURE eat at BROWN'S KEWPEE HAMBURGERS regularly!"

Corresponding pitches in these ads were,

- "When in the mood for really good food, try a Kewpee"
- "Tempting and flavorful...Tastefully Served, Try Our Delicious KEWPEES"
- "The finest suggestion today, Try a Delicious KEWPEE"
- "Just What the Doctor Ordered, A KEWPEE HAMBURGER"
- "TODAY AND EVERY DAY, KEWPEE HAMBURGERS Are the FINEST!"
- "Drop In For That After-Movie Snack."

Advertisements for Brown's Kewpee in Battle Creek, Michigan, featuring panel comics by owner John "Bud" Woolley. *From the* Battle Creek Enquirer, *newspapers.com.*

Advertisements for Brown's Kewpee in Battle Creek, Michigan, featuring panel comics by owner John "Bud" Woolley. *From the* Battle Creek Enquirer, *newspapers.com.*

But in 1963, Woolley was arrested for drunk driving. He was placed on two years' probation and paid a $50 fine and $100 in court costs. He had previous legal problems, which led him to sell the restaurant. The asking price was $16,000, or a leasing arrangement was allowed. He died in 1972 at age sixty-two. In 1973, the abandoned restaurant was slated to be boarded up, and the rear façade of a seven-story office building is on the site today.

Wooley's brother-in-law Melton Bradshaw moved to Jackson in 1961 and operated his Ritzee Hamburger restaurant there before retiring in 1984. His wife, Leah Woolley Bradshaw, worked at Brown's Kewpee from 1955 to 1960 and at Ritzee in Jackson from 1961 to 1984. Leah died in 2005 at age eighty-eight. Melton died a year later at age eighty-seven.

KEWPEE BURGER DRIVE INN IN BELLFLOWER, CALIFORNIA

This is considered to be an outlier Kewpee location, not believed to be authorized by the owners of the Kewpee Hotel trademarks, because it is located far away from the usual Kewpee locations in the Midwest or the Northeast. Bellflower is a suburb of Los Angeles in southeast Los Angeles

County that originally featured orchards and dairy farms, which were overtaken by suburban expansion. It became a city in 1957.

The drive-in was located at 17845 Clark Avenue. It was founded in 1962 and was originally owned by Robert F. Mudlow, who lived in Montebello, California. The grand opening for this drive-in was held from July 13 to July 16, 1962. For the grand opening, it offered the flagship Kewpeeburger, ordinarily forty-nine cents in 1962, for thirty-nine cents. It also had grand opening prices for the regular hamburger, cheeseburger and drink offerings of Coke, orange drink or coffee. In 1965, it was under new management, according to a classified ad published in the *Long Beach Independent Press Telegram* that year, by Walter and Agnes Messler. It claimed in the ad that it offered quality foods, the Best in the West. Along with burgers, it offered barbecue sandwiches, original French dips and pastrami, plus U.S. government–inspected meats. The last ad found for this drive-in was a 1967 classified listing seeking a counter girl. A Google Maps check of the address shows that it is was last occupied by a Tacos y Bionicos Imperio drive-in restaurant that closed permanently.

KEWPEE CAFE IN BENTON, ILLINOIS

Benton is a small town in southern Illinois best known for being the home of U.S. senator and 1884 vice-presidential candidate John Logan, who spearheaded making Memorial Day a national holiday, as well as the boyhood home of actor John Malkovich.

Both men had connections to the Kewpee Cafe in Benton. Logan's home in Benton was next door to the café located at 202 South Main Street, and a historical marker noting where the house used to be is next to where the café once stood. Malkovich, in a 1985 *New York Times Magazine* article titled "The Malkovich Magnetism," mentioned "He also loved whiling away the hours at the Maid-rite and KewPee [*sic*] Cafe listening to the travails of the town, then coming home and imitating what he had heard."

The city grew as its coal mining industry developed. There is a mural of George Harrison of The Beatles to commemorate when he visited the town in 1963 to visit his sister Louise, who was living there at that time. Her husband worked as a mining engineer.

Bob Farmer, in his 2004 self-published book *Lasso the Sunshine: Capture the Brighter Side of Life*, wrote about the town and its Kewpee Cafe in the following passage:

When I was a youngster, I had the good fortune of knowing all four of my grandparents very well. My maternal grandfather, Alan Milton, used to take me with him to work. He used to keep the oil wells maintained and pumping down the back roads of southern Illinois. I vividly remember when I was about eight-years-old stopping by the Kewpee Cafe in Benton, Illinois at six in the morning for Grandpa's breakfast and coffee, but, as I look back, probably more importantly for camaraderie. It was at this local greasy spoon that the blue collar men would gather before work, much like an after work watering hole, but this was for breakfast. Everyone knew my grandpa there, and he knew all of them. They called him "Slim," a nickname earned by his six feet, five inch tall, lanky frame. It did not matter what they ate for breakfast. It only mattered that they were there. It was a collection of various professions, but mostly coal miners. This was the era when coal with king in southern Illinois. So many, including my other grandpa, relied upon it for their livelihoods. Now, unfortunately, the coal industry has left behind abandoned storefronts and only skeletons of abandoned mines as a reminder of the once thriving industry. The Kewpee Cafe held within its walls a collection of hard-working men just trying to make life better for their families and themselves.

The Kewpee Cafe dates to around 1948 and was known at one time as the Logan House Cafe in honor of the house that stood next door. It had a succession of owners over the years, with the earliest known owner being Farrell Sneed, who, upon retirement in 1972, sold the café. It is believed that his daughter Nina Dorchincez acquired it. It was put up for sale again in 1978 when the Dorchincez family moved to Florida, and the owners as of 1981 were Lyman and Margaret Benns. Other owners through the years were Bobbie Fletcher and Marjorie Williams.

When Nina Dorchincez's husband, Gene, suffered a heart attack in Florida, they decided to return to Benton and open a restaurant in 1992 that also doubled as their home called Farrell's, in honor of her father and former Kewpee Cafe owner. Gene died in 2001. Nina died in 2008.

By 2001, the Kewpee Cafe was closed permanently. The site as of this writing is a vacant lot.

KEWPEE IN BENTON HARBOR / ST. JOSEPH, MICHIGAN

The adjacent cities of Benton Harbor and St. Joseph, Michigan, are separated by the St. Joseph River along Lake Michigan in the southwest corner of

Vintage Kewpee Hotel of Benton Harbor ad. *From the* Benton Harbor News-Palladium, *newspapers.com.*

the state. Major appliance company Whirlpool Corporation is headquartered there. But there were other companies that were located there, including Heath Company, noted for its Heathkit electronic kits allowing hobbyists to build their own radios and other products that, after emerging from bankruptcy, moved to Santa Cruz, California, as a scaled-down company. V-M Corporation, which made Voice of Music brand high-fidelity audio equipment, ceased operations in 1977 after filing for bankruptcy.

In 1928, Kewpee Hotel stands opened in both cities operated by Clarence G. Walbridge. After the repeal of Prohibition, the Benton Harbor location was granted a license to serve beer in 1934.

To promote the St. Joseph location at Main and Ship Streets, a series of small square ads a newspaper column wide was published in the *Herald-Press.* They were similar except for the slogan or sales pitch, which included,

- "A Pal To The Palate, That's A Kewpee Sandwich"
- "For a real Hamburg stop at Kewpee Hotel"
- "A loaf of bread, a pound of meat, and all the mustard you can eat. That's a Kewpee sandwich"
- "Kewpee announcement: To our list of sandwiches we are adding hot dogs. Every bite a delight"
- "Boys! Two New Ones In Town! Kewpee Vegetable 10c, Kewpee Deluxe 15c"
- "Mity Nice Hamburgs"

The St. Joseph location was short-lived because a post office was dedicated on the former site of the hamburger joint in 1937. The Benton Harbor location originally at 261 East Main Street at Fifth Street continued with a string of different managers over the years, including G. B. McCloud in 1936, Irwin Stoll in 1938, Edgar Ashley in 1940, Howard Johnston in 1945, Roy Wood in 1947, Maude Schob in 1950 and Roy Woods again in 1952.

In 1946, a fire caused damage to the storeroom and stock in the Benton Harbor Kewpee location. It reopened at a new location at 207 East Main

Street. Another fire struck at that location in 1948, causing a wall to cave in. The cost to replace that wall was $1,500.

By 1951, Walbridge had found a new career as projectionist at the State Theatre in Benton Harbor. Back at Kewpee, the Benton Harbor location through the years had its share of break-ins and burglaries. But in 1952, the janitor who lived in the restaurant's basement foiled a burglary attempt by encountering the intruder who escaped through the same window he used to break in. This was also the last year found that this Kewpee was open.

The restaurant space was vacant for much of the 1950s, except in 1955, when Kewpee briefly reopened, operated by Laura Mack. Another restaurant called the Elbow Restaurant opened by 1958, which was also the year Walbridge died at age sixty-one. But the Elbow Restaurant didn't even last a year, as in December, the building, which was considered an eyesore, was razed to make way for a parking lot between the Vincent Hotel and Gorton's music store, thus putting an end to this part of the Kewpee story.

KEWPEE IN ELKHART, INDIANA

Located east of South Bend on the border with Michigan, the Elkhart area was originally a Native American community. Elkhart is noted for being active in the recreational vehicle and musical instrument industries and in the past had pharmaceutical operations with the maker of Alka-Seltzer and nutritional supplements.

The city directories for Elkhart show that Walter L. Huber had his Kewpee Hotel restaurant as early as 1928 at 115 West Franklin Street. By 1932, Huber had changed its name to Twin Lunch. Sadly, Huber died after a long illness in 1936. His death at age forty may have marked the end of his restaurant. The location today is a parking lot.

KEWPEE IN FINDLAY, OHIO

Findlay, Ohio, in the northwestern part of the state, developed with the area's oil and natural gas industry in the late 1800s. Marathon Petroleum is headquartered there as well as Cooper Tires.

Stub Wilson, who owned the Kewpee Hotel in Lima, Ohio, wanted to open a Kewpee Hotel in Findlay but, after realizing that there was already a Kewpee location there, opened Wilson's Sandwich Shop, which is still in

QUALITY HAMBURG
QUANTITY SANDWICH

* * *

Kewpee Hotel

223 BROADWAY

FINDLAY, OHIO

A 1939 ad for the Kewpee Hotel in Findlay,
Ohio. Because this Kewpee in Findlay
opened first, the Kewpee operator in Lima,
Ohio, opened his Findlay restaurant as
Wilson's Sandwich Shop. *From archive.org.*

Findlay today. Findlay's Kewpee Hotel was located at 223 Broadway and dates, according to material gathered from the "Love Findlay History" Facebook page, to 1930.

The manager at that time was an E.B. Adams. No word as to whether that was Edwin F. Adams, the Kewpee trademark owner from Toledo, in an erroneous listing in the 1931 Findlay City Directory or a relative of his. But the Great Depression had a negative effect on the restaurant, as it was put up for sale in 1932, offering the building and fixtures at half of the original cost.

A later owner was Inez Wittenmyer, who owned it with her husband at that time. After they divorced, Inez married "Shorty" Ferguson, who operated a tree surgeon business, in 1948.

A notable event that took place at the Findlay Kewpee Hotel in 1938 was a wedding held there for Kewpee employees Lucielle Craven and Frank Polorny. To prove it was not a promotional stunt, the wedding was held at three o'clock on a Saturday morning when the restaurant was closed. Among the attendees were former Toledoans Mr. and Mrs. Robert Schnatterly, who also worked at that Kewpee. No word as to who managed the restaurant at that time.

The restaurant was renamed Broadway Sandwich Shop by 1940. In 1955, Bob and Gladys, no surname given, were identified as new owners in a 1955 ad. A 1957 ad for a taxicab company identified Ed Barger as a co-owner. But in 1974, the restaurant was put up for sale. Information could not be found on when it closed, but the building today houses a computer repair shop.

THE KEWPEE ON DORT HIGHWAY IN FLINT, MICHIGAN, NOT CONNECTED WITH HALO BURGER

On December 20, 1978, a new fast-food restaurant with an old name opened in Flint, Michigan, at 573 South Dort Highway between Longway Boulevard and Court Street, which must have caused a lot of confusion. As already mentioned, in 1967 the owner of the Kewpee Hamburgs restaurants

Kewpee Hamburgers Restaurant on Dort Highway in Flint that gave Kewpee spinoff Halo Burger headaches around 1980. *Courtesy of M-Live Media Group.*

in Flint, Bill Thomas, broke away from the Kewpee chain based in Toledo after rejecting the new franchising arrangement demanded by Kewpee owner Edwin Adams, which cost the operators more without giving them more food supplies or advertising support. Thomas changed the restaurant's name to Halo Burger.

Even though the restaurants were called Halo Burger for more than a decade, there were still people at that time who preferred to use their former name of Kewpee. So when a new Kewpee opened on Dort Highway, Terry Thomas, who took over Halo Burger after his father died, fielded calls about this new Kewpee asking if he was part of it and why it was different.

What was different was that this Kewpee was a new franchise authorized by Kewpee's new owners in Toledo since 1977, Robert Dame and Robert Lloyd, who acquired the rights along with some Kewpee locations from Edwin Adams's widow, Hortense. The new Flint franchise, called Kewpee of Flint Inc., was owned by a group of investors led by Grand Blanc builder William Hovey and his wife, Edna (nicknamed Eddy), who oversaw this Kewpee. Bill Thomas was not alone in objecting to Ed Adams's new franchising arrangements. According to Kewpee International co-owner Dame, the number of outlets dropped from sixty to six. In 1979, Kewpee had five company-owned locations in Toledo and franchise operations in four other cities.

The legal entity of Kewpee of Flint Inc. was incorporated on October 25, 1978. Its office was located in a now gone office building at 2051 South

Dort Highway in Flint whose land is currently used as parking by a truck rental business.

This Kewpee location offered the usual fast-food menu items, plus chili and Flint-style Coney Island hot dogs. Along with the indoor dining area, there were three drive-up lanes, with two of them served by an extra kitchen. It was initially managed by Jack Cream, but by 1980, Beatrice Wortman had taken over as manager.

It lasted only a couple of years in Flint, and by 1981, the former Kewpee restaurant building had been remodeled and converted into a Michigan National Bank branch office. The bank closed in the mid-1990s. Over time, the drive-through canopy and former extra kitchen building were razed. More recently, the location served as a used car dealership. As of this writing, it serves as offices for automotive conversion shop Speedo-Metrix.

The Kewpee of Flint legal entity was dissolved on May 15, 1982. William and Edna Hovey relocated to Naples, Florida, in the early 1980s. William died in 1996 at age seventy-one, and Edna died in 2015 at age eighty-seven.

BRIEFLY A KEWPEE IN GRAND LEDGE, MICHIGAN

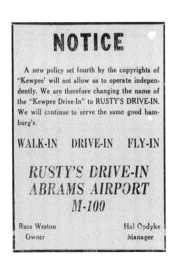

NOTICE

A new policy set fourth by the copyrights of "Kewpee" will not allow us to operate independently. We are therefore changing the name of the "Kewpee Drive-In" to RUSTY'S DRIVE-IN. We will continue to serve the same good hamburg's.

WALK-IN   DRIVE-IN   FLY-IN

RUSTY'S DRIVE-IN
ABRAMS AIRPORT
M-100

Russ Weston   Hal Opdyke
Owner   Manager

Advertising announcing the Kewpee in Grand Ledge, Michigan, changing its name to Rusty's Drive-In. *From the Grand Ledge Independent, newspapers.com.*

In 1946, the city of Grand Ledge, Michigan, located just outside the Lansing area, dedicated the new Abrams Airport. Grand Ledge is noted for its sandstone cliffs, which gave the city its name. In August 1949, Lansing Kewpee co-owner Russell Weston opened a Kewpee drive-in restaurant and sandwich shop there. Grand Ledge's Kewpee marked its grand opening on Saturday, September 17, by offering free root beer.

It lasted only a month before Kewpee trademark owner Ed Adams informed Weston that he would not allow the Grand Ledge Kewpee location to operate as an independent licensee as opposed to being a branch of the Lansing location. So that Kewpee was renamed Rusty's Drive-In, serving the same food as before. No information was found as to how long Rusty's Drive-In was open.

KEWPEE IN GRAND RAPIDS, MICHIGAN

Grand Rapids, Michigan, is known as the "Furniture City" and in more recent years became famous as President Gerald Ford's hometown.

On October 1, 1929, Gerald Boyles opened his Kewpee Hotel hamburger stand at 216 North Division Avenue. At the time he opened his Kewpee, he was a senior at Kalamazoo College. He developed two secret recipes for a burger dressing and onion ring batter. But despite the ill timing of the hamburger stand's founding—the Great Depression started later that month and continued until World War II—the business grew. That hamburger stand was replaced by a modern, full-sized restaurant in 1937.

In 1943, Boyles's brother-in-law A. Arvin Faber joined Kewpee. In 1949, Boyles and Faber expanded the restaurant, adding a processing plant behind it, and bought the Inn We Go restaurant at 2300 South Division Avenue to create a second Kewpee location. Boyles died on February 15, 1958, at age fifty. By 1961, a third location had opened across from the Beltline Drive-in Theatre in the former In Wee Go Drive-in at 1349 Twenty-Eighth Street, which was added onto the following year. Later in 1961, a fourth location was added at 1017 West Leonard.

Opposite: The original Kewpee Hamburgs stand before it was dismantled to make way for the restaurant. *Courtesy of Grand Rapids History Center, Grand Rapids Public Library.*

Above: Kewpee of Grand Rapids 1949 ad for the grand opening of its second Kewpee location and the expansion of the original restaurant. *Courtesy of Jason Mancuso.*

Mr. Fables ad from 1970 showing it still operated a Kewpee location on Division Avenue. *Courtesy of Jason Mancuso.*

Following Gerald Boyles's death, his son John Boyles and John's wife met up with Kewpee trademark owner Ed Adams at his office in Toledo, Ohio, to discuss the Kewpee franchise and trademark agreements. Adams paid visits to Grand Rapids to visit the younger Boyles and see the Grand Rapids Kewpee operations. They had interesting and cordial discussions.

In 1963, John Boyles and John's cousin as well as A. Arvin's son Dick Faber took over the Grand Rapids Kewpee locations. They aspired to open additional restaurants. But concerned with the duration of the Kewpee licensing agreements and geographic restrictions in the agreement and also concerned that there were no geographic protections outside Grand Rapids or Kent County, they established Mr. Fables so they could operate additional locations while plugging the Kewpee locations they still owned. The name was devised by combining Faber's and Boyles's surnames. They continued to use the Kewpee recipes from John's father. Over time, Mr. Fables expanded into a chain of seventeen locations throughout western Michigan. While they added additional Mr. Fables locations, some of the Kewpee locations over time were converted to Mr. Fables. By 1970, only the location at 2300 South Division still identified itself as Kewpee in Mr. Fables' newspaper ads.

The restaurants were cafeteria style, and their popular burgers were the DeLuxe Beefburg, the appropriately named Mr. Fabulous burger and the Oliveburger. They were noted for their onion rings and were the first in the area to serve English muffin bread. By 1988, the chain employed over 650 people and served 25,000 to 30,000 customers daily at locations in Grand Rapids, Wyoming, Kentwood, Standale, Cascade, Muskegon and Holland. They liked to call their operations "upscale fast food" and touted a nicer atmosphere, rather than plastic chairs and tile floors. Their menus also included soups, salads, specialty sandwiches on whole grain buns, fresh pies and chicken and fish dinners.

In 1988, Boyles and Faber sold the Mr. Fables restaurant chain to Fables Innkeepers Management Inc., majority owned by Donald W. Reynolds, including several local investors. In 1990, the original Kewpee location and flagship Mr. Fables restaurant at 216 North Division was sold and was replaced by an office supply store.

In 1995, the chain was sold to Atlanta-based American Family Restaurants Inc., which operated a chain of Denny's restaurants. But they were later sold to an operator that adopted the name Mr. Fables of Nevada, which in 1999 filed for Chapter 11 bankruptcy protection. As a result, the number of locations dropped to six in Grand Rapids and Jenison. Down to three locations in 2000, the last of the Mr. Fables locations closed permanently at 5808 Alpine Avenue NW and 4415 Broadmoor Ave. SE in Grand Rapids along with 155 Chicago Drive in Jenison.

Some of the Mr. Fables locations were converted to New Beginnings family restaurants. But sadly, the secret recipes for Mr. Fables' onion ring batter and the special burger topping are locked up by condiment supplier Litehouse Foods and unavailable. It was written that the Yesterdog restaurant on Wealthy Street in the Eastown area of Grand Rapids, founded by former Mr. Fables employee Bill Lewis, has the rights to the Mr. Fables name and the secret recipes.

In 1960, John Boyles became an attorney, joining a Grand Rapids law firm, and he retired in 2021 after sixty-one years of practice. A. Arvin Faber died in 1977 at age seventy-two. His son Dick Faber died in 2013 at age eighty-three.

Thanks to John Boyles and Jason Mancuso.

KEWPEE IN JACKSON, MICHIGAN

Jackson, Michigan, was named after Andrew Jackson, the seventh president of the United States. Michigan's first state prison was located there in 1838. In 1854, an antislavery meeting was held in Jackson that led to the formation of the Republican Party. Railroad construction led to development of the corset industry there late in the nineteenth century. It became a major automotive manufacturing center in the early twentieth century. Jackson's version of the Coney Island was introduced in 1914 next to a railroad station and became popular with rail passengers. It is the home of CMS Energy, which provides electrical and natural gas service to most of Michigan's Lower Peninsula.

Hamilton "Pat" Patterson was an employee of the Kewpee Hotel hamburger stand in Kalamazoo that was owned by Francis Blair, the son of Kewpee founder Sam Blair. Inspired by the loose-beef Kewpee burger that the Kalamazoo location offered, Patterson moved to Jackson to open his own Kewpee Hotel location, which opened on July 13, 1925.

After about a dozen years of operating his Kewpee Hotel, he married Chicagoan Astrid Teglund. When their restaurant was torn down in the late 1930s, a new brick building was constructed in 1939, which was shared with a barbershop. The Pattersons left the Kewpee fold, and the new Pat's Hamburgs had its grand opening on New Year's Day 1940.

This was mostly a carryout operation. Food was ordered from the counter. There were only four tables in the restaurant along with a pinball machine and a jukebox. It had big bay windows where customers could wait for their orders. But the bulk of their business took place at the drive-through window off the alley. They did their best business on Saturday nights, when more than one thousand burgers were sold.

What was unique about Pat's Hamburgs was the burgers were made on a cast-iron grill. Only hamburgers were prepared on that grill, and it was cleaned only with water—no detergents were used. Anything besides water would ruin its seasoning.

Pat's regular hours were from 9:00 a.m. to 1:00 a.m. Monday through Thursday, 9:00 a.m. to 2:00 a.m. Friday and Saturday and 4:00 p.m. to 1:00 a.m. on Sunday. During World War II, it was closed on Tuesdays due to meat rationing. The Pattersons limited their vacation time to a few days a year on a lake.

But urban renewal meant the end of Pat's Hamburgs, which closed on September 13, 1965, and was torn down afterward. The street was rerouted. The Pattersons chose to retire, stating that they thought they were too old to start over.

In 1925, the Kewpee burgers were five cents. During World War II, with the meat rationing and wartime price controls, the burgers were fifteen cents. When Pat's closed in 1965, regular burgers were thirty cents.

While many people with memories of the Jackson Kewpee/Pat's Hamburgs tried to duplicate the burgers at home, even Pat's wife, Astrid, was unable to duplicate the restaurant's burgers at home.

Hamilton Patterson died in 1977 at age eighty-two. Astrid died in 1980 at age eighty-four.

Kewpee in Kalamazoo, Michigan

The city of Kalamazoo in western Michigan is known for its diversified industries, which over the years included a guitar factory, paper mills, a taxicab factory and the still active pharmaceutical industry. It's also a college town as the home of Western Michigan University.

In 1924, a year after his father opened the first Kewpee Hotel hamburger stand in Flint, Francis J. Blair opened his own Kewpee Hotel hamburger stand in downtown Kalamazoo at 139 East South Street and Burdick Street. The hamburger stand the younger Blair opened looked similar to his father's stand in Flint. But the hamburger the younger Blair developed was so unique that on December 11, 1923, it was issued patent number 26,859 by the United States Patent Office. In 1927, Samuel Wagner was listed as manager. In 1935, Roy Wood was listed as manager. Blair expanded on his father's "We Cater to All the Folks" slogan by adding "at Fairs, Lakes, Shows and Carnivals" and called himself the "Hamburg Sandwich Man."

The original stand was torn down and replaced by a restaurant that opened in January 1937. The restaurant's architecture was similar to designs

The original Kewpee Hotel stand in Kalamazoo before it was replaced by the restaurant a very young Dave Thomas of Wendy's fame dined in. *Courtesy of Kalamazoo Valley Museum.*

commissioned by Kewpee trademark owner Edwin Adams, used by other Kewpee locations, as shown in a 1930 brochure for Pyramid Snap-on Mouldings published by Pyramid Metal Company of Chicago. Quoting from the brochure: "Generous use of Pyramid Metal Mouldings on White Porcelain affords effective display for Kewpee restaurants. An exterior like this brings in the customers." The White Porcelain Mouldings were also used on the interior walls, similar to what survives at the oldest remaining Kewpee location in downtown Lima, Ohio.

Francis Blair developed a hobby of casting aluminum. That led to a successful aluminum casting business that specialized in manufacturing signs and nameplates. So Blair's Kewpee Hotel was sold to Wood in order to concentrate on his casting business. The obituary for Roy Wood's son Richard, who died in 2013, gave the following story: "Growing up, his father owned the Kewpee Hamburg Hotel on South St. in Kalamazoo. In his early years, he worked there until the day he saw a rat behind the counter and announced it to the entire diner, which ended his burger flipping career."

It was this Kewpee location where a young Dave Thomas dined as a child when he lived for a time in Kalamazoo or stayed with his adopted grandmother for the summer. Inspired by that Kewpee as well as the extant location in Lima, Ohio, Thomas used the chain's ideas when he founded his first Wendy's restaurant in Columbus, Ohio, which developed into the large fast-food chain that it is today.

The restaurant closed around 1964 and was torn down shortly afterward. Francis Blair died in 1962 at age sixty-eight.

KEWPEE IN KENOSHA, WISCONSIN

Kenosha, Wisconsin, is located halfway between Milwaukee and Chicago along Lake Michigan. The Chippewa named the area Kenosha, meaning "place of the pike," referring to the annual spawning of trout entering the area rivers from Lake Michigan, thus providing food.

During most of the twentieth century, Kenosha produced automobiles, beginning with the Thomas B. Jeffrey Company in 1902, which was sold to former General Motors executive Charles W. Nash, who renamed it Nash Motors. Nash became American Motors, which was sold to Chrysler. Chrysler closed the Kenosha assembly plant in 1988 and the Kenosha engine plant in 2010.

Today, its location between the Milwaukee and Chicago areas makes Kenosha more of a bedroom community to residents employed in those areas.

In 1929, Hubbel, Michigan native Clifford H. Brunette moved to Kenosha. He acquired the Made-Rite Sandwich Shop at 5703 Sheridan Road shortly afterward. He picked up the rights to the Kewpee Hotel trademarks and made the Made-Rite Sandwich Shop into a Kewpee Hotel location.

In 1930, Brunette got into trouble with the Kenosha Police when they found a slot machine inside the restaurant. So he was charged with operating a gambling device. In the early 1930s, their Kewpee-sponsored baseball teams were either called the Kewpee Hotels or the Kewpees.

In 1934, Brunette was elected secretary of the Kenosha Restaurant Owners' Association. That same year, Brunette applied for a Class B Liquor License. After approval, he opened Cliff's High Life Tavern, which also offered Kewpee Hamburgs. The tavern was location at 1320 Sixty-Third Street.

By 1935, the restaurant and tavern had consolidated to the tavern location on Sixty-Third Street. By 1937, Thomas J. Boyle had taken over the tavern, which lasted through 1939.

Clifford Brunette changed careers by 1939 and became a welder working for the American Brass Company's Kenosha plant; he retired from that factory by then known as the Anaconda Company Brass Division in 1962. He died in 1977 at age eighty.

The Sheridan Road location is today a parking lot. The tavern location on Sixty-Third Street near historic Dania Hall is now a vacant lot.

KEWPEE IN KOKOMO, INDIANA

Kokomo is located in the north-central part of Indiana and was named after Chief Kokomo of the Miami Nation. The discovery of a large natural gas field in the area in the late nineteenth century spurred industrial development of Kokomo, which is still a supplier of automotive parts, with General Motors, Chrysler and BorgWarner as major employers in the area.

In 1929, Wayne Carr was granted a permit to build a small fireproof lunchroom at 116 South Union Street, which was added onto later that year. The following year, Carr started running a series of ads promoting his Kewpee Hotel restaurant in the *Kokomo Tribune*. One ad from June 1930 stated, "After the show or after the dance, a light lunch is a pleasant ending to a pleasant evening. Kewpee Sandwiches are tempting to the palate of all and the high quality of their ingredients insure their deliciousness. Try them tonight. Private parking in rear for customers."

Another ad two months later read, "A Meal In Itself…One might call one of the rich and mammoth Kewpee Hamburgs fried as we fry them here. Cooked on a hot griddle until it reaches the point where it is the easiest to digest and garnished with our own combination of relishes— Your Kewpee Hamburg here becomes a revelation in deliciousness." The same ad stated, "We serve all drinks in sanitary cups," and offered free parking for customers.

The year 1931 brought more ads with new pitches along with a change in ownership. An ad that ran shortly after New Year's Day stated: "Mm m-m Delicious! That's the Popular Verdict of Everybody Who Has Tasted Our Kewpee Sandwiches. Our Kewpee Hamburg and Vegetable Sandwiches are noted for their tasty palatability. Here, too, you get the best quality ingredients in all our sandwiches. Make it a habit to lunch here—you'll like it."

An ad from February 1931 read, "Kewpee Sandwiches, hamburg, ham, vegetable—Are made of quality Meat and Fresh Vegetables. We guarantee prompt and courteous service to everyone at all times. Soft Drinks. Chase &

A 1931 ad for LoVette's Kewpee in Kokomo, Indiana. *From newspapers.com.*

Sanborn Coffee." Along with free parking for customers, the ad made it a point to state the restaurant was "An Authorized Kewpee Hotel."

March 1931 marked a change in management at the Kokomo Kewpee Hotel, as Wayne Carr sold his restaurant to a partnership of Fred P. LoVette and his wife, Cecil. The management change was made clear in an ad for what became LoVette's Kewpee. The LoVettes added catering services, as the ad stated: "Order for your parties. You can serve Lo-Vette's many kinds of tasty Kewpee Sandwiches—hot—at your luncheons and bridge parties. Let us know how many and we will deliver them at your home for the small delivery charge of 25 cents." They made clear in the same ad they offered table service and free parking for customers while they were eating.

A 1937 newspaper article showed that the LoVettes' business partner Churchill Harold was quite talented as an artist and sign painter. Harold was also an inventor who was granted a patent for a bicycle stop light switch activated by the rear brake. Along with partner LoVette, they were building a machine to manufacture the device at sixty per minute and offer it in the marketplace.

Fred LoVette was a native of Battle Creek, Michigan. For the holiday season of 1938, he was visiting his daughter's family in Detroit. On his way back home on December 26, he suffered a stroke and died suddenly in Jackson, Michigan. He was survived by a brother and sister who both lived in Dowagiac, Michigan, and was buried in Dowagiac.

Like some of the other Kewpee locations, the Kokomo Kewpee sponsored a sporting team. In bowling, the Kewpee Hotel quintet finished in fifth place in the regular five-man division of the annual Indiana State Bowling tournament in 1940. In 1941, Kewpee donated to the Greek Relief Fund.

Fred's widow, Cecil, sold the restaurant by 1945 to Fred R. Bolinger. By 1948, Bolinger had changed the name of their restaurant to Fred & Mary's Chili Bowl, which moved across South Union Street to 115 South Union while the Maddox Key Shop was located at the former location.

The year 1948 was the final time that the restaurant was identified in the Kokomo, Indiana city directories. Kokomo's city hall now occupies the old Kewpee location.

Cecil LoVette died in 1957 at age seventy-nine. Fred Bolinger died in 1966 at age sixty-eight. Mary Bolinger died in 2015 at age ninety-two.

KEWPEE IN LA CROSSE, WISCONSIN

La Crosse is located along the Mississippi River and is the largest Wisconsin city on its western border. Its location near the junction of the Black, La Crosse and Mississippi Rivers helped spur its development. Lumbering was a major industry early on. The noted heating and air conditioning company Trane was founded in La Crosse and is still a major employer in the area.

The Kewpee location in La Crosse opened in 1938, offering hamburgers for five cents and hot dogs for a "dime a foot!" according to its ad from that year. It was located at 310 South Fourth Street and was operated by Arthur Grathen and his brother-in-law Harry Volkel. Grathen was born in Winona, Minnesota, located about thirty miles southeast of La Crosse along the Mississippi River, and started in the restaurant business there at age seventeen. He liked it so much that he acquired his own restaurant in 1929. He operated the Kewpee Hamburger Shop in Winona and decided to partner in the new Kewpee venture in La Crosse. He sold his interest in the Winona Kewpee around 1940. The La Crosse Kewpee sponsored a women's bowling league that won the 1942 city women's team championship.

During World War II, this Kewpee became a gathering place for soldiers from Camp McCoy. Grathen recalled in a 1971 interview that there were nine people working on a shift, and "you didn't dare open Saturday morning until all nine were there."

The bulk of Kewpee's business by that time was farmers, as the farmer's market at that time was located across the street. Weekdays brought about downtown workers eating lunch there.

A 1938 ad for the new Kewpee in La Crosse, Wisconsin. *From newspapers.com.*

By 1948, its address was 314 South Fourth Street. In 1960, it offered carryout hamburgers at ten for $1.00 and $0.10 each for extras beyond ten on Sunday only from 1:00 a.m. to 7:00 p.m. In 1963, it had a carryout special that September with a free six-pack of Pepsi-Cola with every ten hamburgers at the carryout price of $1.49 plus tax and bottle deposit. Extra burgers were $0.15 each. So this Kewpee seemed to follow the "buy 'em by the sack" pitch that noted burger chain White Castle became famous for.

Grathen bought out Volkel in 1964, but by that time, a bad knee was slowing him down. But as is often stated, all good things had to come to an end. After thirty-two years of operation, Kewpee of La Crosse owner Arthur Grathen closed his restaurant for the final time on Saturday, August 28, 1971. He decided that after forty-two years in the restaurant business, he felt that was enough. He decided to take it easy for a while and thought he would work part time for his son's freight line business.

Arthur Grathen died on January 12, 1973, at age sixty-one at a local hospital. His funeral was in La Crosse, and he was buried in Winona. His obituary was published in both the La Crosse and Winona newspapers. His La Crosse Kewpee partner Harry Volkel died on March 5, 1975, at age seventy-five. He also previously lived in Winona, and his obituary was published in both newspapers. Arthur's widow, Dorothy, died on January 22, 1984, at age seventy-two, and Harry's widow, Esther Grathen Volkel, died on February 20, 1990, at age ninety.

KEWPEE IN MUNCIE, INDIANA

The city of Muncie, Indiana, grew in the 1880s with the natural gas deposits found in the area, which led to several industries being located there, most notably glass manufacturing.

On April 18, 1929, the *Muncie Evening Press* reported that a new hamburger stand called "the Kewpee Hotel" was being built next door to the newspaper's office. Located on 117 South High Street, it was reported at that time that it was one of a chain of twenty-five or thirty such establishments that operated in the north-central states. Contractors from nearby Elkhart built that Kewpee.

The *Evening Press* reported in the May 23, 1929 issue that Kewpie doll creator Rose O'Neill authorized and was executing the design of signs for the Kewpee chain of restaurants. This included the Kewpie doll mascot design on the new Muncie location that opened a week before the May 23 report was published.

A month later, the June 24, 1929 issue gave rave reviews and noted that the new hamburger stand was attracting hundreds of patrons because of the excellent food quality and speedy service. The speedy service was helped by the limited menu. Along with hamburgers, it also offered a special orange drink, all kinds of soft beverages, milk—what the article called "the best coffee in the city"—home-made pies and candy. The article concluded that "the quick service, combined with the clean surroundings and the hygienic handling of the food makes it a pleasure to drop into the Kewpee Hotel for a lunch at any time."

Charles E. Kirkwood was the owner of the Muncie Kewpee Hotel. He was spotlighted in an article in the May 5, 1930 issue of the *Muncie Morning Star*, which was co-owned with the *Evening Press*. The article in that paper stated that "Mr. Kirkwood insists on quality in everything he serves. Good

KEWPEE HOTEL
NOW OPEN

Featuring

Kewpee Sandwiches

We Cater to All the Folks.

117 So. High Street

Next to "Press" Building

A 1929 ad for the Kewpee Hotel in Muncie, Indiana. *From newspapers.com.*

hamburgers are relished by most people, and those at the Kewpee Hotel will meet the taste of the most fastidious and be served in an appetizing manner." The same article noted the large parking area for the hamburger stand's drive-in service.

Both newspapers published additional articles praising the hamburger stand next door, where it was assumed that the staff of both papers spent many a lunch hour. But by 1937, Kirkwood had decided to drop the Kewpee Hotel franchise because it got too expensive. It was first called Kirk's Famous Hamburgers before holding a contest to give the restaurant a new name. In his January 12, 1989 column, *Muncie Star* columnist Bill Spurgeon credited Gene Carter with the winning new name, the Hi-Hat.

Hi-Hat Hamburgers continued to be a popular hangout spot with Muncie patrons, which also included students at Ball State. In 1949, Kirkwood retired and sold his restaurant to longtime employee and manager Edward E. Himes. Himes was previously spotlighted by the *Morning Star* on January 29, 1943, when he and his brother Ora were inducted into the armed forces—Ora on March 24, 1941, when he was stationed in the Hawaiian Islands, and Edward on January 25, 1943, at Fort Benjamin Harrison.

On Saturday evening, April 16, 1950, members of the Sewing Club threw a farewell party for C. Edwin Kirkwood and his wife, Maude, at a cabin in Heekin Park. The Kirkwoods had announced plans to move away from the Muncie area on Wednesday and settle in California. Long tables were set up, decorated with spring flowers. Following dinner, a gift was presented to the Kirkwoods, and the twenty or so guests played bridge and canasta afterward.

Under Eddie Hines's ownership, the Hi-Hat continued to prosper. But on Wednesday morning, January 27, 1960, Jess Nolley drove with his Hi-Hat employee-wife Dorothy to the restaurant to drop her off. His car's headlights caught an image of Hines inside the building with his head to one side. He told his wife not to enter and drove to the police station to mention something was wrong at the restaurant. Police had to force open a door to enter the building and found Hines hanging from a length of clothesline rope suspended from overhead water lines. He had stepped off a stool that remained standing a few inches from his body. Hines, who was forty, had in recent months slept on a cot at the extreme rear of the building.

The doctor estimated that Hines died by strangulation at 5:00 or 5:30 a.m., leaving behind his son Carl, his daughter Deanna, three brothers and five sisters. The funeral was held the following Friday at Meeks Mortuary with the Reverend Frank Stevenson officiating. He was buried at Hawk Cemetery.

Hines's suicide death was a total shock to the staff of the *Muncie Star* and *Muncie Evening Press* who were regular lunchtime customers of the former Kewpee restaurant next door. According to the *Star*, "Eddie Himes was a congenial man who liked people and he had the faculty of employing waiters and waitresses who had this same quality. The result was that food, fellowship and fun were found in the Hi-Hat. The clientele included not only newspaper folks, but numerous students from Central High School, workers in offices in the area, and others who made a point to drop in when they were in the vicinity."

"Eddie Himes had worked in this restaurant since he was a young man and he eventually bought it from his employer and had operated it successfully for years. In his death we have lost a friend, a man who liked to cook, especially those dishes his patrons preferred. He enjoyed their patronage and his association with them."

The Hi-Hat continued to operate for the first few months of 1960; then the two newspapers bought the building and tore it down the following June to make way for an addition housing the circulation department.

In 1976, Kewpee/Hi-Hat founder C. Edwin Kirkwood relocated from California to Racine, Wisconsin, where he lived to the ripe old age of ninety-nine, passing away on April 4, 1994.

In 2018, the three-structure *Muncie Star Press* complex was sold to Ivy Tech Community College. That included the former site of the Kewpee/Hi-Hat restaurant. The buildings were torn down to make way for the college's three-story George & Frances Ball Building, which opened in 2019.

KEWPEE IN NILES, MICHIGAN

Just north of the Indiana state line and South Bend is the city of Niles. In 1930, Jesse Marlin and his wife, Lettie, established Marlin's Kewpee Hotel Restaurant at 215 South Eleventh Street in Niles. They lived next door to the restaurant at 219 South Eleventh Street. After Prohibition was repealed, this Kewpee Hotel began serving beer. So over the years, this restaurant was often identified as Marlin's Kewpee Tavern.

While several Kewpee restaurants did not survive World War II because of meat shortages, this Kewpee got in trouble in 1944 for violating rationing regulations. As a result, it was suspended from dealing in meats, canned fish and cheese for ninety days by the Office of Price Administration, which during the war was in charge of rationing commodities that were in short supply.

By 1950, the address was slightly altered to 211 South Eleventh Street. The Kewpee restaurant/tavern closed in 1963. Lettie died in 1965 at age sixty-nine. Jessie was seventy-six when he died in 1970. A Google Maps check shows the former Kewpee location now occupied by a commercial building constructed in 1984, which on last check was occupied by a check cashing service, a used car dealership and a tire store.

KEWPEE IN PONTIAC, MICHIGAN

Located between Detroit and Flint, Pontiac, Michigan, was named after the chief of the Ottawa Nation who led a war against the British in 1763, attempting to capture Fort Detroit. In the twentieth century, it had major automotive operations of General Motors, and its now defunct Pontiac brand was based there.

By 1929, Barrett Harrison had a Kewpee Hotel at 21 North Perry Street. By 1931, he had opened a second Kewpee Hotel location at 33 West Lawrence Street. By 1935, Harrison had left the Kewpee fold and changed the name of the restaurants to Lawrence Lunch. J. Benjamin Niemie was the manager of the Lawrence Street location, and Harrison was running the Perry Street location. No further information was found about the restaurants. The locations are now parking lots.

KEWPEE IN PORTSMOUTH, OHIO

Announcing

H. L. "Buck" Buchanan

NOW OPERATING

Kewpee Hotel

Corner 6th and Gay Sts.

Featuring:
*A Mity Nice Hamburg
and Light Lunches*

A 1936 ad for the Kewpee Hotel in Portsmouth, Ohio. *From newspapers.com.*

Located along the Ohio River across from Kentucky, the city of Portsmouth, Ohio, briefly had a Kewpee Hotel for about a year, owned by Harry L. "Buck" Buchanan. Also alongside Portsmouth is the Scioto River, which feeds the Ohio River.

It opened in February 1936. But it ran into bad luck a few months later as a flood nearly covered the entire restaurant. In February 1937, Buchanan contracted with a builder to remodel the restaurant, which would have all new fixtures. Sporting new plastered walls, it reopened the following month. But when it reopened in March 1937, it reopened under a new name, the Tip Top Sandwich Shop. No further information could be found regarding how long the Tip Top Sandwich Shop was in business.

KEWPEE IN SANDUSKY, OHIO

Sandusky, Ohio, is located along Lake Erie between Toledo and Cleveland. It is best known as the home of the Cedar Point amusement park.

On September 14, 1939, Don White Sr. and his two sons opened a Kewpee Hotel restaurant, billed as "Sandusky's newest sandwich restaurant." It sold Kewpee hamburgs for ten cents and the deluxe hamburg for fifteen cents. It offered a full line of beverages, chili, frosted malteds, pies, rolls and cereals. Note that like many other Kewpee locations in the early years, French fries were not offered.

Like many Kewpee restaurants that opened in the 1930s, it had white enameled steel paneling on the exterior trimmed in orange. Located at the corner of Wayne and East Market Streets, its entrance was at the corner of the building with the naked Kewpie statue above it. At night, long gooseneck lamps lit up the white façade. There was also a neon sign saying "HAMBURGS" on the roof above the Kewpie statue. Patrons inside the restaurant could watch their food being prepared, as the grill was in full view.

By 1943, the Sandusky Kewpee Lunch was being operated by Chester D. McMillan. A few years later, it was taken over by Carl and Helen Ruth.

The Kewpee location in Sandusky, Ohio. *Sandusky Library Research Center.*

They sold it in 1954 to Lyle Mayhew, who left the Kewpee fold and changed the restaurant's name to the Whitehouse Restaurant. The only other change besides the name was the Kewpie statue was taken down. The manager of the restaurant after the Ruths took over was Lyle's brother-in-law Roger Markley.

Eventually, Markley took over that restaurant and changed the name of it to Markley's. Around 1964, he extensively renovated the restaurant and moved the entrance from the building's corner to the Market Street side of the building.

Markley's closed in 2010, and two years later, a Subway franchise took over the building and still occupies it today, sharing the space with Amarone Italian restaurant. While the exterior is still basically the same as when it was Markley's, a small addition was added on the Market Street side.

KEWPEE IN SOUTH BEND, INDIANA

Along the St. Joseph River, South Bend, Indiana's location attracted industries, including Oliver farm implements and Studebaker carriages, which evolved into manufacturing tractors and motor vehicles, respectively. While Oliver and Studebaker are long gone, there is still AM General, which manufactures specialty motor vehicles such as the Humvee. AM General evolved from Willys-Overland Motors, which introduced the Jeep utility vehicle.

From the 1920s through the 1950s, members of the Harper family owned and operated the Kewpee Hotel Hamburgs location, which, as a hamburger stand, moved in its early years, and the Harper family also endured tragedy.

Ernest E. Harper opened his first Kewpee Hotel hamburger stand on South St. Joseph Street, forty-four feet from Jefferson East. A 1926 ad boasted that the drive-in was only a few steps from the center of town. It also stated, "All sanitary methods of serving are employed by us." Along with "clean, sweet, plump and pretty hamburgs," it also served "satisfying and refreshing" Kewpee Orangeade.

By 1928, the stand had moved to 311 North Michigan Street. It boasted that the establishment was "where Notre Dame men meet," as South Bend is home to the University of Notre Dame. By that time, it also offered hot and cold drinks plus "Mexican Chile and Hot Tomale."

A 1930 news story about a robbery at Kewpee indicated that it relocated to 323 North Michigan Street.

The first tragedy that struck the Harper family was when Ernest Harper's wife, Grace, died of injuries received in an auto accident in 1937. She was fifty-four. Her husband filed a negligence lawsuit against the driver of the car Mrs. Harper rode in, seeking $10,000 against the driver, identified as John Hook.

Two years later, Ernest Harper died suddenly while visiting his daughter in Kalamazoo, Michigan. He was sixty-three. Ernest's son Forrest M. Harper took over running the South Bend Kewpee Hotel.

In 1940, Forrest Harper bought an old house built by the late Joseph Warden, who owned the South Bend Woolen Company, and last occupied by Dr. E.P. Moore. The house was directly across North Michigan Street from Kewpee Hotel Hamburgs. The house was torn down, and a new larger Kewpee Hotel Hamburg was built at 328 North Michigan Street. One exterior feature was a lighted tower. For the grand opening, it offered souvenirs for the kiddies. It was open twenty-four hours a day, offering sirloin

The Kewpee location in South Bend, Indiana. *Courtesy of St. Joseph County Public Library.*

hamburgers, frosted malts and a complete fountain for drinks along with drive-in service and indoor dining. It even had jukebox coin-operated remote selectors installed in each booth playing the latest song and dance hits.

The new location proved so successful that Forrest Harper threw a Christmas party for his employees that year in the Oldenburg Inn, five miles south of South Bend. He presented gifts, and there was socializing after dinner.

By 1941, this Kewpee, by that time identified as Harper's Kewpee Hamburgers, offered a "burger in a basket" for twenty-five cents. That was described as "a tasty hamburger on a toasted bun, smothered with french fries and surpassed by none." The ad also plugged the restaurant sponsoring "Prep School Grid Edition" each Wednesday night on a local radio station.

In 1942, Harper's Kewpee Hotel Hamburg sponsored an invitational basketball tournament at the South Bend Armory. Unfortunately, the Kewpee Bees team did not win and lost the consolation game to finish fourth in the tournament.

Tragedy struck the Harper family again in 1943 when owner Forrest Harper, recently inducted into the army, died of a heart attack in Camp Lee, Virginia. This left his widow, Irene, in charge of the South Bend Kewpee.

In 1947, Irene Harper expanded the Kewpee's parking lot, offering more drive-in spaces. It had additional openings for carhops, fountain operators, another waitress and an extra dishwasher.

Like many other Kewpee locations, the exterior of the restaurant included a large statue of a naked Kewpie doll. In 1947, the girlfriend of Kewpee patron Joseph Pesci dared him to put a diaper on the statue. The local news story from May 27, 1948, reported that Pesci found material suitable for a large diaper and attached the diaper to the statue. That gained him seventeen dollars and three dinners.

Another news story from April 3, 1951, found the people of South Bend to be caring enough to help motorists in distress. A family of ten found that their 1929 pickup truck broke down. South Bend police offers showed they had bigger hearts than their badges. An auto repair shop fixed the truck for no charge. South Bend officers collected enough money to feed the family at the Kewpee Hotel restaurant. Owner Irene Harper prepared a gallon of hot soup, a dozen hamburgers, French fries, crackers, cookies, milk and coffee. She refused to accept money for the food.

The Kewpee location was remodeled in 1952. That summer, it was closed Tuesdays and Sundays so employees could enjoy those days off. But all good things have to come to an end. Irene Harper placed one final ad in the local paper on August 23, 1957, stating, "It is with real regret that we at Kewpee's say 'Good-Bye' to our many, many friends and customers. We have discontinued business as of August 20."

Today, North Michigan Street is Dr. Martin Luther King Jr. Boulevard. An office building now occupies where Kewpee once stood at 328 North Dr. MLK Jr. Boulevard.

KEWPEE IN TOLEDO, OHIO

For decades, Kewpee was based in Toledo, Ohio, along Lake Erie near the Michigan border. A strip of land including Toledo was the subject of a territorial dispute between the State of Ohio and Michigan Territory in 1835–36 that became known as the "Toledo War." President Andrew Jackson signed a settlement giving the Toledo Strip to Ohio and giving Michigan the Upper Peninsula. Michigan became a state in 1837. The city of Toledo grew with the completion of the Erie Canal. It became known for its glass industries and also has an automotive presence, such as with Chrysler's Jeep assembly plant.

When Edwin Adams opened his Kewpee Hotel hamburger stand in downtown Toledo in 1926 and acquired the rights to the Kewpee Hotel trademarks from Samuel Blair, he had ambitions to make it a regional chain of hamburger joints. He opened restaurants as far east as Utica, New York, as well as licensed other operators to open Kewpee Hotel locations.

When he decided to expand into a restaurant, he commissioned a standard design for Kewpee Hotel restaurants as described in a flyer published by the Pyramid Metals Company of Chicago for their Pyramid Snap-On Mouldings. In describing the interior and exterior designs, the flyer stated, "Generous use of Pyramid Metal Mouldings on white porcelain affords effective display for Kewpee restaurants. An exterior like this brings in the customers." The flyer credited owner E.F. Adams, Toledo, Ohio. That location was in downtown Toledo at 314 North Erie Street.

Around 1937, Adams opened a second Kewpee location at 2248 Monroe Street northwest of downtown. That restaurant's later design showing art deco influence still survives at the licensed Kewpee restaurant in downtown Lima, Ohio.

Over time, it seemed that Adams was spreading himself too thin, as he began closing far-flung locations as early as the mid-1950s. The Utica location was becoming run-down, so it was sold and became a Burger King.

Adams maintained Kewpee Hotel's executive offices in the ten-story United Savings Building, built in 1924 at 519 Madison Avenue in downtown Toledo. It is now known as the Huntington Bank Building.

In 1964, Adams opened his third Toledo Kewpee location at 2515 West Laskey Road not far from Whitmer High School in the far northwest side of town near the Michigan state line.

But in 1967, Adams made the mistake of his life by demanding a full franchising arrangement and a percentage of the profits without providing additional advertising support. As a result, the number of Kewpee locations dropped from sixty to six.

On July 6, 1974, Adams was visiting his daughter in Tulsa, Oklahoma, when he died suddenly at age sixty-nine, leaving his widow, Hortense, to run the company. In 1977, she sold her Kewpee restaurants and the rights to the Kewpee trademarks to two real estate developers who owned apartment buildings, Robert L. Dame and Robert J. Lloyd. They acquired all franchise rights, patents, trademarks and logotypes of Kewpee International.

A new company called Kewpee Inc. of Toledo was formed. It would operate company owned locations at 314 North Erie Street downtown and 2515 West Laskey Road with plans to remodel both locations. Dame and Lloyd closed the location at 2248 Monroe Street and Collingwood Boulevard. They announced the individual restaurants would continue to grind their own beef daily and hamburgers would be cooked to order.

Vintage 1978 ad for the Kewpee locations in Toledo, Ohio. *Courtesy of the OldToledo Facebook page.*

Dame and Lloyd announced that they would be franchising additional Kewpee locations. One Kewpee they franchised did open in 1978 at Kewpee's founding location in Flint, Michigan, which must have caused headaches at Halo Burger, the former Flint Kewpee restaurants, as several Flintities still referred to Halo Burger as Kewpee even today. As previously mentioned, that outlier Kewpee in Flint lasted only a couple of years.

In short order, a third Kewpee location opened at 3201 Navarre. In 1979, a fourth location opened at 3435 Secor Road. It was decorated with a movie theme, and for the ribbon cutting, instead of a ribbon, a string of burger buns was cut.

Also in 1979, a fifth Toledo-area Kewpee location opened at 6201 Monroe Street west of U.S. 23 in the suburb of Sylvania with 2,450 square feet of floor space and parking for sixty vehicles.

When Adams started Kewpee in Toledo, he offered in 1926 $0.05 hamburgers and frosted malteds. In a 1981 review of the Toledo Kewpee locations, along with the burgers, which were $0.99 for a single, $1.75 for a double and $0.59 for a junior, it also offered a salad bar and "kewpons" (what they called coupons) for deals that included in 1981 fish and chips on Wednesdays for $0.99 and $1.50 off any $5.00 purchase if you returned the following week for a kewpon.

But in the 1980s, the chain started its decline. Maybe it was new restaurant competition. The Kewpee-influenced and growing Wendy's chain did not help. In any case, the final Kewpee location closed in 1985, and the trademarks and franchising rights to Kewpee were transferred to the management of the Lima, Ohio Kewpee restaurants.

Of the Kewpee locations with identified addresses, the downtown Kewpee on Erie Street is now a parking lot. The location at 2248 Monroe Street is now a vacant lot. The location at the corner of West Laskey & Douglas is now a gas station. A bank now stands where the Kewpee once stood on Navarre. A jewelry store is now where Kewpee was on Secor Road. That jewelry store, I understand, is in a renovated former Wendy's restaurant, which has this writer thinking that Wendy's replaced Kewpee at that location. The Kewpee location that was at 6201 Monroe Street in Sylvania is now the location of a Kroger supermarket.

After selling her Kewpee restaurants and trademarks, Hortense Adams moved to Arizona, where she died in 2001 at age ninety-six. She is interred next to her husband in the Sanctuary of Light mausoleum, East Abbey, east wall at Ottawa Hills Memorial Park in Toledo.

KEWPEE IN UTICA, NEW YORK

Utica, New York's growth in the early nineteenth century was boosted with the completion of the Erie Canal.

In 1938, Kewpee rights owner Edwin Adams opened a Kewpee Hamburgs in Utica at 1300 Genesee Street at Plant Street. The business was legally incorporated on July 6, 1939, in New York as Kewpee Hotel Co. Inc. It was built using the standard Kewpee design at that time with the Kewpie statue above the entrance and white enameled paneled exterior and interior walls.

As a teenager, noted literary critic and poet Albert Spaulding Cook worked part time at this Kewpee location. He recalled he worked the weekend night shift there while in high school.

It looked identical to the oldest-surviving Kewpee location in downtown Lima, Ohio. It became a major hangout spot for Utica's young people and was considered to be the equivalent to Arnold's from the TV sitcom *Happy Days*.

Its patrons included students from nearby schools Utica Freedom Academy, St. Francis de Sales School and Utica College. Along with the Kewpie statue, old patrons recalled the neon sign that read, "Please do not blow horn. Use lights for service." It had small jukebox selectors in each indoor booth as well as carhops for outdoor patrons who would serve food in trays hung from rolled-down car windows.

But all good things have to come to an end, and changing times led this Kewpee location to be torn down in 1973 to make room for a Burger King. A Dunkin' Donuts occupies the site today.

Lima, Ohio Kewpee operator Harrison Shutt recalled in 1993 that two years before, he and his wife traveled to Utica to deliver a chest filled with

Kewpee burgers to someone who requested some. Shutt recalled that the requester was like a little kid when they met at the hotel Shutt was staying in. Even though Utica was a nine-hour drive from Lima, the burgers in the center of the chest were still warm. Their visit to Utica was even covered by the local newspaper there.

KEWPEE IN WINONA, MINNESOTA

Winona, Minnesota, is located along the Mississippi River and developed around a settlement called Keoxa, occupied by a Mdewakanton band of the Dakota Sioux Nation. Immigrants from New England and Europe began settling there in 1851. Winona was named after Princess Winona, a daughter of a Dakota chief who, the story goes, chose suicide rather than marry a suitor she did not love. The town's location along the Mississippi, still a major shipping artery, spurred its development.

The Winona Kewpee story begins with Arthur Grathen, the Winona native already mentioned in the earlier piece about the Kewpee location in La Crosse, Wisconsin. It was around 1927 that the seventeen-year-old Grathen began his career working in a restaurant. Two years later, he was running his own restaurant, which, in a 1930 article regarding an auto accident he was involved in, seemed to be one of the many imitations of the successful White Castle restaurants. This one in Winona was the White Shop System hamburger stand. It was located at 151 East Third Street.

In the March 19, 1934 issue of the *Winona Daily News*, it was announced that Grathen and his partner Felix Sadowski severed their connection with the White Shop hamburger stand and would open another hamburger shop in the next ten days or two weeks at 126 East Third Street. That was the new Kewpee Hamburger Shop. But in 1937, tragedy stuck when Arthur Grathen's father, Nicholas Grathen, died of bronchial pneumonia at the home of one of his daughters after being bedridden for a week at age sixty-seven. Out of respect for the memory of Arthur's father, the Kewpee location was closed for an hour between 9:30 a.m. and 10:30 a.m. on Saturday, January 6.

In 1940, the Kewpee hamburger shop moved to a new location at 151 East Third Street in the former White Shop System location. But the grand opening was spoiled by vandalism in which a glass cutter was used to make a crack the full height of the new restaurant's front window, causing sixty dollars in damage. By that time, Arthur Grathen picked up a new partner with his brother-in-law Harry Voikel. Shortly afterward, Grathen and Volkel

"Something New at the KEWPEE LUNCH!"

NOW — ANYTIME — DAY OR NIGHT
YOU CAN HAVE AN ORDER OF

BATTER FRIED CHICKEN

● If you like chicken prepared the way it's really good . . . then you'll like it here. Fried in deep fat and encased in golden brown batter. Chicken and toast **30**c

OUR BATTER FRIED CHICKEN IS PREPARED IN A NEW, ULTRA-MODERN FRIER — THAT'S WHY IT'S SO GOOD.

●

Eat It Here or Take It Out - Quick Service

●

KEWPEE LUNCH

CORNER THIRD AND WALNUT STS.   TELEPHONE 2237

A 1942 ad announcing the addition of fried chicken to the menu of the Kewpee location in Winona, Minnesota. *From newspapers.com.*

sold the Winona Kewpee to concentrate on their Kewpee location thirty miles or so upstream along the Mississippi in La Crosse, Wisconsin.

The new owners of the Winona Kewpee were Edward G. Rivers and his wife, Florence. In 1942, they expanded their menu by offering batter-fried chicken, fried in deep fat and encased in golden brown batter. They offered it for thirty cents back then, either in the restaurant or takeout.

A 1943 news story in the *Winona Daily News* revealed what became of the old White Shop System hamburger stand. Thomas "Bernie" Monahan and his son Dean operated that White Shop location before leaving Winona to join the U.S. Merchant Marine, seeing service during World War II. Dean was serving as a head cook aboard a cargo ship. His previous civilian experience included being a cook at restaurants in Rochester and St. Paul, Minnesota. After serving sixteen months at sea, the two returned to Winona for R&R (rest and relaxation). While Bernie was staying at a hotel, Dean became a patient at Winona General Hospital to be examined before returning to his troop transport ship.

Back at Kewpee, it was granted a "mechanical device license" in 1943. There was no mention regarding whether it was a jukebox or a pinball machine. This Kewpee location also sponsored a bowling team called the Kewpee Lunches, which won the citywide midseason tournament in 1944.

Fire broke out above the Kewpee restaurant in the upstairs apartments in 1944, causing twenty residents to flee and causing $5,000 in damage. The first-floor tenants, including Kewpee Lunch and Kewpee Annex, had only minor damage. With another fire affecting this Kewpee the following year, it can now be determined that the "mechanical device license" was a jukebox. A short circuit in that jukebox resulted in a fire at that Kewpee caused $150 in damage to the jukebox and $300 in damage to the restaurant. The 1945 news story about the second fire indicated that fuse was burned out, but electricity was on again in a short time.

In 1946, a new Kewpee Annex was opened around the corner from the main restaurant in the same building, constructed in 1886, with the address being 160 Walnut Street. This afforded the Winona Kewpee considerably better accommodations and facilities for handling customers.

This Kewpee continued to sponsor bowling teams, taking part in the Night Owl women's bowling league in 1947. Kewpee co-owner Florence Rivers served as vice president of that league. Also in 1947, the Kewpee Lunch & Annex added a new walk-in storage freezer measuring 12 by 18 by 7.5 feet. In 1950, Kewpee of Winona sponsored two competing bowling teams representing Kewpee Lunch and Kewpee Annex. The Kewpee Lunch squad defeated the Kewpee Annex squad that year in the Class A league of the Winona Athletic Club. The winning Kewpee Lunch team consisted of Earl Kane, J.C. Page, Clarence Rivers, Ralph Benicke and O.F. Koetz, with team manager W.T. Joswiak.

In 1965, the fire department was called to the Kewpee location due to smoke from a stoker backing up. Fortunately, there was no fire. Later in 1965, the restaurant dropped from the Kewpee fold and changed its name to Goodie's Corner, named for the restaurant's corner location at Third and Walnut Streets. They had an all-you-can-eat fish special for $1.25 every Friday that year from 5:00 p.m. to 9:00 p.m.

By that time, Edward and Florence Rivers had sold the restaurant. Edward then became an agent at the Greyhound Bus Depot. He was semiretired and working part time at the Greyhound station when he died of a heart attack in 1980 at age seventy-five. Florence Rivers died in 1995 at age ninety-one.

Today the former Kewpee location houses the Winona Community Day Center in the same nineteenth-century building.

9

A VISIT TO TWO HISTORIC KEWPEE LOCATIONS

Two Kewpee locations are still in operation and are considered historic landmarks. The oldest in Flint was not built as a Kewpee but became one in 1951. It left the Kewpee fold, becoming a Halo Burger in 1967, and is a treasured fast-food landmark today. The other is a fine example of art deco design and is the oldest-surviving Kewpee location built as a Kewpee in downtown Lima, Ohio. This author visited the locations.

THE LAST REMAINING FORMER KEWPEE IN THE FOUNDING CITY OF FLINT, MICHIGAN

This piece was adapted from Gary Flinn's book *Remembering Flint, Michigan: Stories from the Vehicle City.*

A deliciously different culinary aspect of Flint history that continues to this day began in 1929. That was when a two-story Mediterranean-style building with stuccoed walls, arched windows and a tiled roof was built by the Vernor's Ginger Ale Company. It's located downtown at 800 South Saginaw Street and was the company's retail store and sandwich shop, serving the bubbly beverage whose "deliciously different" flavor was aged four years in oak barrels. A notable feature was an electric sign that depicted in light bulbs a bottle of Vernor's ginger ale being poured into a glass. There was also a warehouse on the site, where many oak barrels filled with Vernor's ginger ale syrup were stored, waiting for the flavor to mellow. Barrels were even stored in underground tunnels between the warehouse and the sandwich shop. One customer who recalled going there was Charles Weinstein, who as a child bought Vernor's ginger ale for his father, Morris Weinstein, who didn't want to be seen patronizing the rival business, as he co-owned the M&S Beverage Company.

In 1932, sign painters John Gonsowski and Keith Martin, working for General Signs, painted a three-story advertising mural for Vernor's on the north wall of the Sharp Hardware & Implement Company building next door, later known as the Peerless Mattress & Furniture Company building, which faces the Vernor's sandwich shop. Gonsowski was born in Poland and came to Michigan in 1913. He showed his European sensitivities in regard to his painting style. He painted smiling Vernor's gnomes working out of a castle, stacking oak barrels that say "flavor mellowed 4 years in wood" on the mural. Gonsowski painted other Vernor's advertising signs throughout the Flint area. In 1951, Vernor's moved the oak barrels from the site, and James Vernor II sold the sandwich shop to Bill Thomas, the manager of Kewpee Hamburgs, a downtown Flint fixture since 1923 that was located

The landmark downtown Flint Halo Burger (the former Vernor's Outlet) and the sole surviving former Kewpee run by Bill Thomas. *Author photo*.

at 415 Harrison Street. Vernor's took down the pouring bottle sign, and Bill Thomas erected a neon Kewpee sign with the Kewpie doll logo.

The Kewpee Hotel (the "Hotel" would later be dropped to avoid confusion from customers who thought the business offered lodging instead of hamburgers) was founded, as mentioned earlier, by Samuel V. Blair, who was nicknamed "Old Man Kewpee" or the "Hamburger King." He was a colorful man who claimed that he originated the flat bun and invented the "deluxe" hamburger. Before arriving in Flint in 1923, he had been an iron molder for thirty years, sold vacuum cleaners and life insurance, studied horticulture and operated orchards. He opened the first Kewpee Hotel at 415 Harrison Street in a wagon-like building. Legend has it that it was buried on the site when it was replaced by a real building, which had numerous renovations over the years and was torn down in 1979. For Kewpee Hotel's twentieth anniversary in 1943, he gave that day's customers war savings stamps.

William V. "Bill" Thomas came to Flint in 1933 and started working for Blair in 1938. On April 1, 1944, Thomas took over management of the Harrison Street restaurant, leasing the restaurant from Blair, who retired. Characteristically, Blair threw a big retirement party for himself, inviting several friends. Blair died in 1945. The two downtown Flint Kewpees were not the only ones. Why the Kewpee restaurants were called Hotels are lost to history. At its peak, there were more than two hundred Kewpee restaurants before World War II. The early Kewpees were not franchises, and there was no group association. Each differently owned Kewpee had its own menu with its own different style of hamburger. Bill Thomas took full ownership of the Flint Kewpee Hamburgs in 1958, but as already mentioned, the ownership rights to the Kewpee name Blair sold to Ed Adams of Toledo in 1926. In the early 1960s, Adams wanted to switch from a flat royalty fee to a full franchising arrangement. In 1967, Adams demanded a percentage of the profits from each Kewpee in place of the licensing fees without providing additional support. Because Bill Thomas did his own advertising and promotion for his Kewpee restaurants, he decided to change the name. So on May 12, 1967, the Flint Kewpee restaurants were renamed Bill Thomas's Halo Burger restaurants. Only the name changed. Everything else, including the food, remained the same.

After Vernor's sold the sandwich shop to Bill Thomas, the maintenance of the Vernor's mural next door stopped. Over the years, it started to become faded. Bill Thomas wanted to fix it up, but the owner of Peerless Mattress resisted having the mural maintained. It wasn't until the Greater

Inside, the old Vernor's outlet's interior was preserved including the "V" for Vernor's design on the ironwork. *Author photo.*

Flint Arts Council's Urban Walls Committee, which commissioned murals in downtown Flint, stepped in wanting to restore the Vernor's mural that Peerless Mattress finally agreed. Halo Burger donated $27,000 for the restoration of the mural in 1979, which included two additions to the mural in place of blank wall space. The restoration and addition were done by Donna Devantier and Michael Perry of Eller Outdoor Advertising. Original artist John Gonsowski was on hand during the restoration. On the large mural addition to the right of the original mural, a small extension to the castle, an open field and houses in the background were added. As a tribute to Halo Burger, a cow with a halo over its head was painted on the large mural addition. Halo Burger's mascot is an angelic cow. After the mural was completed, the mural was coated with a sealant to protect it. When Vernor's built the sandwich shop, it included a small building or a "guardhouse" and gates for the delivery trucks to go through. The small building was at one time Pete's Diner run by Peter Parascos. Through the years, it also housed May's Lunch, Tom's Lunch and Thomas' Pantry Shoppe. It finally became storage before it was torn down to aid in the mural restoration and provide additional parking for Halo Burger. The small mural addition that occupies where the small building stood features a painted guardhouse for the castle with a winking gnome looking through the window.

In 1995, the Peerless Mattress building was gutted in an arson fire, which forced Peerless to move to the suburbs. The Vernor's mural was undamaged, but the building the mural was painted on was threatened. Fundraising to buy the building and fix it up was successful, saving it from demolition, and the Greater Flint Arts Council moved into the former Peerless Mattress building. In 2001, the mural received a second restoration. Steve Davidek and Stephen Heddy (both of whom also worked on a mural restoration in the Genesee County Court House) worked on the second restoration of the Vernor's mural, which was funded by the Ruth Mott Foundation. In 1979, the owner of Vernors did not help with the first restoration. But for the second restoration, Dr Pepper/Seven Up Inc., which took over Vernors in 1994, contributed funds to help in the second restoration.

Over the years, the Halo Burger location that was formerly Vernor's and Kewpee had additions built, which are faithful to the building's original design.

The display case with Halo Burger memorabilia including trophies for teams Halo Burger sponsored. *Author photo.*

The Flint Kewpee locations pioneered drive-through takeout windows. The original Kewpee/Halo Burger was torn down in 1979 to make room for parking for the new University of Michigan–Flint downtown campus.

Vernors lost the apostrophe in its name when the company went public following the death of James Vernor III in 1957 at age thirty-nine because the company needed additional capital. The Vernor family reluctantly sold the ginger ale company in 1966 because of estate tax problems dating back to the death of James Vernor II in 1954.

The old Kewpee slogan is "Hamburg pickle on top! Makes your heart go flippity-flop!" Halo Burger's slogan is "Seven days without a Halo Burger makes one weak."

This piece could not have been completed without the assistance of the following people, whom I give many thanks to: Randy Farb, of blessed memory, of the Flint Public Library; Greg Fiedler of the Greater Flint Arts Council; Terry Thomas at Bill Thomas's Halo Burger; and Karen Kassel, who is the great-granddaughter of original Vernor's mural painter John Gonsowski.

Inside the flagship Halo Burger, other than the modern counters, equipment and menu board monitors, it still looks like the old Vernor's outlet down to the intricate plaster and tile work, original light fixtures and a sign stating "Practice—Counter Service Only." Both inside and outside, there are Vs on the ironwork standing for Vernor's. The Coca-Cola fountain on the self-serve counter includes Vernors among the drink choices.

THE OLDEST-SURVIVING KEWPEE RESTAURANT, IN LIMA, OHIO

As previously mentioned, Stub Wilson opened his Kewpee Hotel hamburger stand in downtown Lima, Ohio, in 1928. Originally with an enclosed but exposed to the elements walk-up service window, the counter was completely enclosed the following year.

As Lima grew over the years, so did its Kewpee hamburger stand. In 1939, a new design for the Kewpee Hamburgs restaurant was devised. Kewpee owner Edwin Adams decided to open a company-owned location in Utica, New York. Stub Wilson replaced his hamburger stand with a full-sized restaurant. Both new restaurants shared the same design featuring a porcelain enameled finish that was beginning to become popular at gasoline stations.

The interior of the oldest-surviving Kewpee restaurant in Lima, Ohio, is a time capsule, looking pretty much like it originally looked in 1939. *Author photo.*

By comparison, a 1957 photo of the downtown Lima Kewpee's interior. *Courtesy of Kewpee Inc.*

The new Lima Kewpee introduced malts to the menu served in a frosted soda glass and eaten with a spoon. That may have influenced Wendy's Frosty. While this new Kewpee originally had curb service, it switched to having a drive-through window. But due to the narrow parking area, the rear of the parking lot featured a turntable allowing vehicles to be rotated 180 degrees in order to exit the parking lot. The turntable was abandoned around 1957 when a building next door was torn down allowing for expanded parking.

Inside what is now the oldest-surviving Kewpee restaurant built as a Kewpee, it is like going into a time capsule. The walls still have the porcelain enamel finish. On each corner on either side of the restaurant's front exit are the familiar naked Kewpie statues similar to the large Kewpie statue greeting patrons above the entrance. It is truly a historic landmark in Lima, Ohio.

AFTERWORD

W hy were the second-oldest hamburger restaurant's numbers reduced
to five locations in three cities? The reasons are numerous. For
example, there was no standard chain-wide menu. The Olive Burgers that
Old Man Kewpee introduced at his very first Kewpee Hotel hamburger
stand in Flint consists of loose olives that are still served at Halo Burger
locations in Mid-Michigan. At Weston's Kewpee in Lansing, fourth-
generation operator Autumn Weston's great-grandmother and Canadian
immigrant Gladys Johnson Weston Bowlin created her olive sauce that is
served with that Kewpee's award-winning Olive Burger.

While World War II meat shortages did reduce the number of Kewpee
locations in the 1940s, as the decades progressed, changes in restaurant
ownership also reduced the number of Kewpee locations. But in the mid-
1960s, it was the general greediness of Kewpee rights owner Ed Adams that
caused the number of Kewpee locations to drop considerably.

As the number of franchised fast-food hamburger restaurants increased,
the resulting competition also led to the drop in the number of Kewpee
restaurants. But as for the remaining Kewpee locations, a devoted customer
base and the quality of the food drive in the business.

At the landmark oldest-surviving Kewpee location in downtown Lima,
Ohio, built in 1939, there is a lineup of cars waiting for their turn at the
drive-through window during the lunch hour on North Elizabeth Street,
which is a one-way street—the city posts signs on how to angle park. The

The Vernor's mural next to the downtown Flint Halo Burger (former Kewpee) parking lot. *Author photo.*

restaurant's own parking lot was once so narrow that a turntable was used at the back of the lot for cars to turn around.

Even older is the former Kewpee of Flint No. 2, which was built in 1929 as the Vernor's ginger ale outlet store and sandwich shop at 800 South Saginaw Street. In 1951, Vernor's sold the shop to Flint Kewpee owner Bill Thomas, who changed the name of his hamburger restaurants to Halo Burger in 1967. It still serves Vernors ginger ale. During the summer months, a Boston Cooler made with vanilla ice cream and Vernors ginger ale is a cool refreshment. This is now the flagship location of Halo Burger and is a Mediterranean-style architectural jewel of a landmark in downtown Flint flanked by a historic Vernor's ginger ale advertising mural featuring Vernor's mascot gnomes on the other side of the downtown Flint Halo Burger's parking lot.

KEWPEE LOCATIONS IDENTIFIED WITH ADDRESSES IF KNOWN

(Locations in boldface are still in operation)

CALIFORNIA

BELLFLOWER
Kewpee Burger Drive Inn
17845 Clark Avenue (Walter and Agnes Messler, owners)

ILLINOIS

BENTON
Kewpee Cafe
202 South Main Street

ELGIN
Kewpee's Colonial Drive Inn
802 Villa Street

PEORIA
604 Main Street

INDIANA

ELKHART
115 West Franklin Street

FORT WAYNE
219 West Jefferson (Frank Anderson, manager)

HAMMOND
5235 (615) Hohman Avenue (G.W. Webb, manager)

KOKOMO
116 South Union Street

MARION

MISHAWAKA
105 North Mill (Maurice W. Reed, manager)

MUNCIE
119 South High Street (C.K. Kirkwood, manager)

SOUTH BEND
South St. Joseph Street
109 North Mill Street
311 North Michigan Street
323 North Michigan Street
327 North Michigan Street
(Michigan Street is now Dr. Martin Luther King Jr. Boulevard)

Kewpee Hotel
HAMBURGER
Always in the Crowd | We Cater To All Folks
115 W. FRANKLIN ST.

KEWPEE HAMBURG SYSTEM
604 Main Street
We Deliver   Phone 4-8077
The Largest and Classiest
Hamburgers in Peoria

Left: A 1929 ad for the Kewpee Hotel in Elkhart, Indiana. *From archive.org.*
Right: A 1932 ad for the Kewpee Hotel in Peoria, Illinois. *From archive.org.*

KENTUCKY

LOUISVILLE
1801 Portland Avenue (Ethel A. Bennett, owner)

MICHIGAN

ANN ARBOR
514 East Liberty
South and East University

BATTLE CREEK
59 West State Street

BENTON HARBOR
261 East Main Street
207 East Main Street

BUCHANAN
(Herbert Allee and Richard Rogers, co-owners)

CROTON TOWNSHIP (Newaygo County)

EAST LANSING
325 East Grand River Avenue (Jean's Kewpee/Ralph's Kewpee/Spiro's Cafeteria)

FLINT
415 Harrison Street (converted to Halo Burger)
800 South Saginaw Street (converted to Halo Burger and only surviving former Kewpee in Flint)
573 South Dort Highway (not connected with Halo Burger)

GRAND LEDGE
Abrams Airport
16815 Wright Road

GRAND RAPIDS (CONTINUED ON NEXT PAGE)
216 North Division Avenue
2300 South Division Avenue

GRAND RAPIDS (CONTINUED)
1349 Twenty-Eighth Street
1349 South Division Avenue
(The four listed Kewpee locations in Grand Rapids were converted to Mr. Fables.)

HAMBURG (Livingston County)

JACKSON
107 Cooper Street (renamed Pat's Hamburgs)

KALAMAZOO
139 East South Street at Burdick

LANSING
115 West Shiawassee Street
5559 South Pennsylvania
6525 South Pennsylvania
118 South Washington (still in operation)

MACKINAW CITY

NILES
211 South Eleventh Street

A 1930s vintage photo of Mackinaw City, Michigan, showing the Kewpee Hotel Hamburgs on the right. *Courtesy of Vintage Michigan Postcards and Timothy Bowman.*

PONTIAC
33 West Lawrence Street
21 North Perry Street

SAGINAW
413 Federal Avenue

ST. JOSEPH
Main and Ship Streets

MINNESOTA

WINONA
126 East Third Street
151 East Third Street
160 Walnut Street (Kewpee Annex)

NEW YORK

UTICA
1300 Genesee Street, Oneida Square

OHIO

AKRON
15 South High Street

FINDLAY
223 Broadway

LIMA (Kewpee's current home base, all locations open)
111 North Elizabeth Street
2111 Allentown Road
1350 Bellefontaine Avenue

PORTSMOUTH
Sixth and Gay Streets (H.L. "Buck" Buchanan, manager)

SANDUSKY
East Market and Wayne Streets

SYLVANIA
6201 Monroe Street at US-23

TOLEDO
314 North Erie
2248 Monroe and Twenty-Third Street
2515 West Laskey Road and Douglas Avenue
3201 Navarre Avenue
3435 Secor Road

TROY

WISCONSIN

KENOSHA
5703 Sheridan Avenue
1320 Sixty-Third Street (Cliff's High Life Tavern)

LA CROSSE
310 South Fourth Street
314 South Fourth Street

RACINE
520 Wisconsin Avenue (open)

BIBLIOGRAPHY

Books and Periodicals

American Weekly. "Headache Honeymoon of Mr. Blair, Hamburger Hero." September 7, 1941.

Batura, Paul J. *Chosen for Greatness: How Adoption Changed the World.* Washington, D.C.: Regnery Faith, 2016.

Danielson, Kay Marnon. *South Bend, Indiana* (Images of America). Charleston, SC: Arcadia Publishing, 2001.

Farmer, Bob. *Lasso the Sunshine: Capture the Brighter Side of Life.* Self-published, 2004.

Flinn, Gary. *Remembering Flint, Michigan: Stories from the Vehicle City.* Charleston, SC: The History Press, 2010.

Grant, Tina, ed. *International Directory of Company Histories.* Vol. 156. Farmington Hills, MI: St. James Press, 2014.

Hogan, David G. *Selling 'em by the Sack: White Castle and the Creation of American Food.* New York: New York University Press, 1997.

Kindman, Michael. *My Odyssey Through the Underground Press: Voices from the Underground.* East Lansing: Michigan State University Press, 2011.

Lewis, Norma. *Lost Restaurants of Grand Rapids.* Charleston, SC: The History Press, 2015.

Massie, Larry B., and Peter J. Schmitt. *Kalamazoo, The Place Behind the Products.* Woodland Hills, CA: Windsor Publications, 1981.

McMillian, John. *Smoking Typewriters: The Sixties Underground Press and the Rise of Alternative Media in America.* New York: Oxford University Press, 2011.

Mollison, Andre W. "Hollander's Dark And Milder Stream." *Michigan State News* 58, no. 147 (May 1966): 2.

Myers, Sharon Moreland. *Classic Restaurants of Summit County.* Charleston, SC: The History Press, 2018.

"New and Remodeled Hotels." *Hotel Monthly* 34, no. 401 (August 1926): 88.

Peavey, Sandra Vincent, and the Terry Wantz Historical Research Center. *Newaygo County 1920–2000* (Images of America). Charleston, SC: Arcadia Publishing, 2014.

Powell, Mary Alice. "Dining Out—A Guide Before You Order." *Toledo Blade*, March 13, 1981.

Pyramid Metals Company. *Pyramid Snap-On Mouldings*. Chicago, Pyramid Metals Company, 1930.

Shutt, Harrison. "Kewpee Hamburgers' History." *Allen County Reporter* 49, no. 1 (1993):14–43.

Thomas, R. David. *Dave's Way: A New Approach to Old-Fashioned Success*. New York: G.P. Putnam's Sons, 1991.

Toledo Blade clippings from the Toledo Public Library's scrapbooks covering Kewpee stories from 1977 to 1979.

United States Patent Office. *Index of Patents Issued from the United States Patent Office, 1923*. Washington, D.C.: Government Printing Office, 1924.

Internet Articles

Company Man. "White Castle—Why They're Successful." YouTube. https://www.youtube.com/watch?v=IQIqqiZ3LVE.

Friess, Steve. "How Halo Burger Found Its Purpose amid the Flint Water Crisis." Fast Company, May 9, 2017. https://www.fastcompany.com.

Greco, Rachel. "After 40 Years at Kewpee's, Tammie Bunker Is at the Heart of Lansing Eatery." *Lansing State Journal*, December 5, 2022. https://www.lansingstatejournal.com.

Horsman, Tom. "History by Horsman: Kewpee and Markley's." *Sandusky Register*, February 17, 2021. https://sanduskyregister.com.

Karpus, Mike. "Sorry Folks, I Can't Pry Loose the Fables Secret." *Grand Rapids Press*, September 11, 2008. https://www.mlive.com.

Martinez, Shandra. "Mr. Fables Co-Founder Remembered for More than Mr. Fabulous Burger." *Grand Rapids Press*, December 24. 2013. https://www.mlive.com.

PastFactory. "The Story of Kewpee Hamburgers: One of America's Original Fast Food Restaurants." https://www.pastfactory.com.

Rent, Andy. "What Do You Think? Would You Like Mr. Fables to Return?" 100.5 The River. https://rivergrandrapids.com.

Smith, Leanne. "Peek Through Time: Cast-Iron Grill Was the Secret to Tasty, Simple Loose-Meat Burgers at Jackson's Pat's Hamburgs." *Jackson Citizen-Patriot*, September 13, 2022. https://www.mlive.com.

WCRZ Cars 108. "Flint's Iconic Downtown Halo Burger Set to Reopen After a Year Closed." https://wcrz.com.

ABOUT THE AUTHOR

Gary Flinn is a product of the Flint (Michigan) Community Schools and a graduate of Mott Community College and Michigan State University who lived in the Flint area most of his life. His earliest writings were for Flint Central High School publications *The Tribal Times* and *The Arrow Head*. He also contributed articles for the *Uncommon Sense*, *Your Magazine*, the *Flint Journal*, *Broadside* and *Downtown Flint Revival* magazine. He presently lives on Flint's west side.

Also by Gary Flinn from The History Press

Hidden History of Flint
Lost Flint
Remembering Flint, Michigan: Stories from the Vehicle City

The author at the historic Kewpee restaurant in downtown Lima, Ohio. *Photo by Ivonne Raniszewski.*

Visit us at
www.historypress.com
....